Quality 15.95

W9-CBE-178

QUICK COURSE®

in

MICROSOFT®

Excel 2000

Fast-track training® for busy people

JOYCE COX
POLLY URBAN
CHRISTINA DUDLEY

PUBLISHED BY
Online Press
15442 Bel-Red Road
Redmond, WA 98052
Phone: (425) 885-1441, (800) 854-3344
Fax: (425) 881-1642
E-mail: quickcourse@otsiweb.com
Web site: www.quickcourse.com

Publisher's Cataloging-in-Publication
(Provided by Quality Books, Inc.)

Cox, Joyce.
   Quick Course in Microsoft Excel 2000 / Joyce
Cox, Polly Urban, Christina Dudley. -- 1st ed.
   p. cm. -- (Quick Course books)
   Includes index.
   ISBN: 1-58278-003-X

   1. Microsoft Excel for Windows.   2. Business--
Computer programs.   3. Electronic spreadsheets.
I. Dudley, Christina.   II. Urban, Polly.   III.
Title.   IV. Title: Microsoft Excel 2000   V.
Series.

HF5548.4.M523C69 1999   005.369
               QBI99-500178
                  99-070317
                  CIP

Printed and bound in the United States of America.

1 2 3 4 5 6 7 8 9 I P I P 3 2 1 0

Content overview

Content details

PART ONE: LEARNING THE BASICS

PART TWO: BUILDING PROFICIENCY

ONE

LEARNING THE BASICS

Part One covers the basics of Excel, giving you a strong foundation on which to build your skills. In Chapter 1, you learn to navigate your way through the program as you create a simple table. Then in Chapter 2, we show you how to edit and format the table, and introduce you to Excel's templates. Finally, in Chapter 3, you explore some of Excel's built-in functions while learning various ways to perform calculations with your data. As a final step, you print your worksheet and publish it as a Web page.

1

Getting Started

To learn the basics of Excel, you build a simple table for tracking sales by invoice. You learn how to input information into Excel by entering different types of data, how to give Excel instructions, and how to save and retrieve files.

You can easily adapt the worksheet you create in this chapter to track any source of income, including membership fees or donations.

Worksheet created and concepts covered:

Enter numeric
values as text

Enter and format column
headings to give worksheet
tables structure

Set up the toolbars
to suit the way
you work

Assign a specific
date format

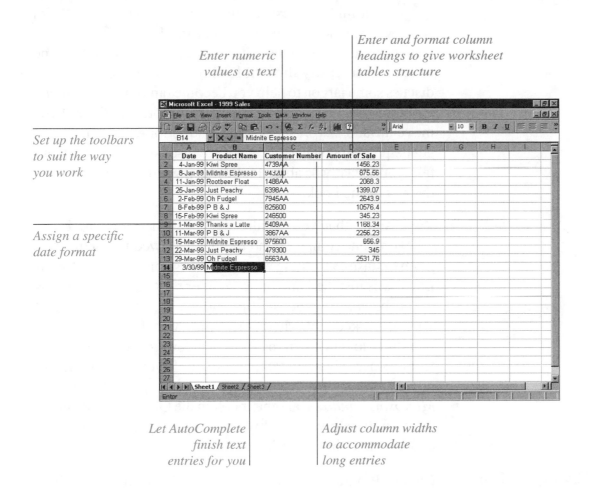

Let AutoComplete
finish text
entries for you

Adjust column widths
to accommodate
long entries

At first glance, Microsoft Excel 2000 can seem pretty intimidating, especially if you've never worked with a spreadsheet program before. But like most software programs, Excel loses its scary aura if you take the time to learn it in easily digestible chunks. In this chapter, we discuss some jargon to help you become familiar with Excel's terminology. Then we cover how to enter text and numbers, move around a worksheet, give instructions, save files, and get help when you need it. After we discuss these fundamentals, you'll easily be able to follow along with the examples in the rest of the book.

We assume that you've already installed Microsoft Excel 2000 on your computer and that you allowed the Setup program to stash everything where it belongs on your C: drive. (If Excel was installed on your computer by a network administrator, be sure to read the tip below.) We also assume that you've worked with Microsoft Windows before and that you know how to start programs, move windows, choose commands from menus, highlight text, and so on. If you are a Windows novice, we suggest that you take a look at *Quick Course® in Microsoft Windows*, another book in the Quick Course series, which will help you quickly come up to speed. Well, that's enough preamble, so let's get going:

Different configurations

We wrote this book using a computer running Microsoft Windows 98 with the screen resolution set to 800x600. If you are using a different version of Windows or a different resolution, you might notice slight differences in the appearance of your screens. We are also using the Excel configuration that results when you do a Typical installation of Microsoft Office 2000 from CD-ROM. Don't be alarmed if your setup is different from ours. You will still be able to follow along with most of the examples in this book.

1. Choose Programs and then Microsoft Excel from the Windows Start menu.

2. If necessary, click the Office Assistant's Start Using Microsoft Excel option. (We discuss the Office Assistant in more detail on page 25. As you work your way through this chapter, the Office Assistant—an animated paper-clip object called Clippit—may entertain you with some cute antics and may occasionally display a message or use a light bulb to indicate that it has a comment to make about your current activity. Other than admiring its animations, you can ignore it for now.) Once the program is loaded, your screen looks like the one shown at the top of the facing page.

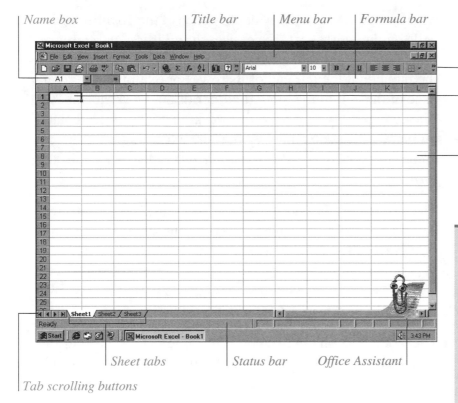

Name box | Title bar | Menu bar | Formula bar

Toolbars

Active cell

Worksheet

Sheet tabs | Status bar | Office Assistant

Tab scrolling buttons

To reduce screen clutter and increase the size of the program's window, let's turn off the Windows taskbar:

1. Click the Start button, click Settings, and then click Taskbar & Start Menu (Windows 98) or Taskbar (Windows 95 and Windows NT).

2. In the Taskbar Properties dialog box, click the AutoHide check box to select it, and click OK. If necessary, click the program window's title bar to make the window active. The taskbar disappears, and the program window expands to fill up the newly available space.

3. Point to the bottom of the screen to make the taskbar temporarily reappear, and then move the pointer away from the bottom of the screen to hide the taskbar again.

Taking up the majority of the screen is a blank *worksheet*, which, as you can see, is laid out in a grid of *columns* and *rows* like the ledger paper used by accountants. There are 256 columns, lettered A through IV, and 65,536 rows, numbered 1 through 65,536. The rectangle at the junction of each column

Other ways to start Excel

Instead of starting Excel by choosing it from the Start menu, you can create a shortcut icon for Excel on your desktop. Right-click an open area of the desktop and choose New and then Shortcut from the shortcut menu. In the Create Shortcut dialog box, click the Browse button, navigate to C:\ Program Files\Microsoft Office\ Office\excel, and click Open. Click Next, type a name for the shortcut icon, and click Finish. For maximum efficiency, you can start Excel and open an existing workbook by choosing the document from the Documents submenu of the Start menu, where Windows stores the names of up to 15 of the most recently opened files. If you are using Microsoft Office 2000, you can also choose Open Office Document from the top of the Start menu and navigate to the folder in which the workbook you want to open is stored. If you want to start Excel and open a new workbook, you can choose New Office Document from the top of the Start menu and then double-click the Blank Workbook icon.

Cell addresses →

and row is called a *cell*. To identify each of the 16 million plus cells on the worksheet, Excel uses an *address*, or *reference*, that consists of the letter at the top of the cell's column and the number at the left end of its row. For example, the reference of the cell in the top left corner of the worksheet is A1. The *active cell*—the one you're working with—is designated on the worksheet by a heavy border. Excel displays the reference of the active cell in the *name box* at the left end of the *formula bar*.

The *status bar* at the bottom of the window displays useful information. As you'll see later on page 71, the status bar includes an *AutoCalculate area*, where Excel displays the sum of entries in selected cells.

An Overview of Workbooks

The worksheet on your screen is just one sheet in the current file, which is called a *workbook*. By default, each new workbook contains three sheets. However, a single workbook file can contain as many as 255 sheets, named Sheet1 through Sheet255. You can have several types of sheets in one workbook, including worksheets, chart sheets (where you create graphs of worksheet data), and macro sheets (where you store automated ways of manipulating data). This workbook format allows you to store related data on separate sheets but in a single file. (We don't use any macro sheets in this book, but if you're interested, you can read about macros in Excel's Help feature. See page 24 for information about how to use Help.)

Sheet tabs →

For each sheet in a workbook, Excel displays a *tab*, like a file-folder tab, above the status bar at the bottom of the screen. These tabs are handy for moving from sheet to sheet. Try this:

Displaying sheets →

1. Click the Sheet2 tab. Excel displays that sheet.

2. Next click the Sheet3 tab to display that sheet, and finish by selecting Sheet1.

Entering Data

Most worksheets consist of tables of numbers, called *values* in spreadsheet jargon. You perform various calculations on these values using equations, which are called *formulas*. You can also enter dates, times, and text. (Dates and times are considered values because you can use them in calculations; see the tip on page 12.) In this section, you'll get the ball rolling by entering some text, values, and dates in a simple worksheet for a fictional ice cream company called *Cream of the Crop*. You'll see how to enter formulas in Chapter 3.

As you'll see in the next section, you can complete your entries in the worksheet's cells in several different ways. For the sake of convenience, we've summarized these ways in the table below:

To do this...	Use this...
Stay in the same cell	Enter button
Move down	Enter key or Down Arrow
Move up	Shift+Enter or Up Arrow
Move right	Tab key or Right Arrow
Move left	Shift+Tab or Left Arrow

Entering Text

To make your worksheets easy to read, you usually enter text as column and row headings that describe the associated entries. Let's try entering a few headings now:

1. With cell A1 selected, type *Date*. As you type, the text appears in both the cell and the formula bar, and a blinking insertion point in the cell tells you where the next character you type will be inserted. A Cancel button (✗) and an Enter button (✓) appear between the formula bar and name box. Meanwhile, the indicator at the left end of the status bar changes from Ready to Enter because the text you have typed will not be recorded in cell A1 until you "enter" it.

2. Click the Enter button to complete the entry. Excel enters the Date heading in cell A1, and the indicator changes to Ready. The entry is left-aligned in its cell. (Unless you tell Excel to do otherwise, it always left-aligns text.)

3. Click cell B1 to select it. The reference displayed in the name box changes from A1 to B1.

Entering headings

The tab scrolling buttons

The number of sheets in the workbook may exceed the number of tabs Excel can display at the bottom of the worksheet window. You can use the tab scrolling buttons to the left of the Sheet1 tab to bring the tabs for hidden sheets into view, without changing the active sheet. Click the First Sheet or Last Sheet button to display the tabs for those sheets and the Previous Sheet or Next Sheet button to move tabs into view one at a time.

4. Type *Product Name*, but instead of clicking the Enter button to enter the heading in the cell, press the Tab key. Excel completes the entry in cell B1 and selects cell C1.

5. Type *Customer Number* and press the Tab key.

6. Now enter one more heading. In cell D1, type *Amount of Sale* and click the Enter button to complete the entry. This is how the newly entered row of headings looks in the worksheet:

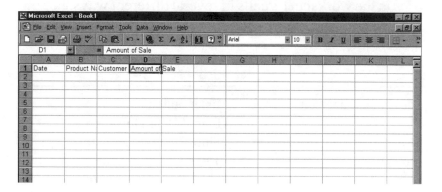

Long text entries

Notice that the headings in cells B1, C1, and D1 are too long to fit in their cells. Until you entered the Customer Number heading in cell C1, the Product Name heading spilled over into C1, just as Amount of Sale spills over from D1 into E1. After you entered the Customer Number heading, Excel truncated Product Name so that you could read the heading in C1. The Product Name and Customer Number headings are still intact, however. (If you're skeptical, click either cell and look at the formula bar.) After you have entered more information, you'll adjust the column widths to accommodate long entries (see page 19).

That completes the column headings. Now turn your attention to the rest of the table. You'll skip the Date column for now and enter the names of a few ice cream flavors in column B:

1. Click cell B2 and type *Kiwi Spree*.

2. Instead of clicking the Enter button, press the Enter key. Excel completes the entry in B2 and selects B3.

3. In cell B3, type *Midnite Espresso* and press the Enter key to complete the entry and move to cell B4.

Changing what the Enter key does

If you want the Enter key to move your selection in a direction other than down, choose Options from the Tools menu and click the Edit tab. Below the Move Selection After Enter check box, click the arrow to the right of the Direction edit box, make your selection, and click OK. To specify that the active cell should remain active when you press Enter, deselect the Move Selection After Enter check box.

4. Next type the following names in the Product Name column, pressing the Enter key after each one:

B4   *Rootbeer Float*
B5   *Just Peachy*
B6   *Oh Fudge!*

5. In cell B7, type *P*. Excel anticipates that you'll type *Product Name*. When you type the first characters of an entry already in a column, Excel's AutoComplete feature finishes the entry for you. If Excel's entry is correct, simply move on to the next one. This entry is not correct so complete it by typing a space and then *B & J* and pressing Enter.

◄──────── AutoComplete

6. Continue with the following entries, pressing Enter when Excel's entry is correct:

B8   *Kiwi Spree*
B9   *Thanks a Latte*
B10   *P B & J*
B11   *Midnite Espresso*
B12   *Just Peachy*
B13   *Oh Fudge!*

Entering Numbers as Text

Now let's enter the customer numbers in column C. Normally, you want Excel to treat customer numbers—and social security numbers, part numbers, phone numbers, and other numbers that are used primarily for identification—as text rather than as values on which you might want to perform calculations. If the "number" includes not only the 0 through 9 digits but also letters and other characters (such as hyphens),

Correcting mistakes

If you make a mistake, you can simply click the cell containing the error, type the new entry, and press Enter. If you want to correct part of an entry, you can also edit the entry directly in its cell. Click the cell and press F2, or double-click the cell. Then press Home or End to move the insertion point to the beginning or end of the entry and press Right Arrow or Left Arrow to move the insertion point forward or backward one character. Press Backspace to delete the character before the insertion point or Delete to delete the character after the insertion point. Then type the correction and click the Enter button.

Pick From List

In addition to AutoComplete, Excel offers another option to save you time typing text entries. Right-click the next cell in a column and choose Pick From List from the shortcut menu to display a list of the entries you've already typed. You can then select the next entry from the list rather than typing it.

Excel usually recognizes it as text. However, if the number consists of only digits and you want Excel to treat it as text, you have to explicitly tell Excel to do so.

For demonstration, assume that the Cream of the Crop company sells ice cream to both large chain stores and individually owned ("mom and pop") stores. All stores are denoted by a customer number with six characters. The customer numbers for large chain stores consist of four digits followed by the letters AA, and the customer numbers for individually owned stores consist of six digits that end with 00 (two zeros). Try this to see how Excel treats these customer numbers:

1. Click cell C2, type *4739AA,* and press the Enter key. This customer number consists of both digits and letters, so Excel treats the entry as text and left-aligns it.

2. In cell C3, which is now active, type *943200* and click the Enter button. This customer number consists of only digits, so Excel treats the entry as a value and right-aligns it.

Using apostrophes

How do you tell Excel to treat an entry that consists of only digits as text? You begin the entry with an apostrophe ('). Follow these steps:

1. In cell C3, type *'943200* and press Enter. (When you type the new entry, Excel overwrites the old entry.) Because of the apostrophe you typed, Excel recognizes the new entry as text.

2. Enter the customer numbers shown below in the indicated cells, preceding those that end in 00 with an apostrophe so that Excel will treat them as text:

C4	*1488AA*
C5	*6398AA*
C6	*7945AA*
C7	*'825600*
C8	*'246500*
C9	*5409AA*
C10	*3867AA*
C11	*'975600*
C12	*'479300*
C13	*6563AA*

Formatting numbers as text

You can make Excel treat an existing value as text by selecting the cell containing the value, choosing Cells from the Format menu, and on the Number tab, selecting the Text format and clicking OK. You can also format values as zip codes, phone numbers, and social security numbers by selecting Special on the Number tab and then selecting the appropriate Type option.

The results are shown in the screen below:

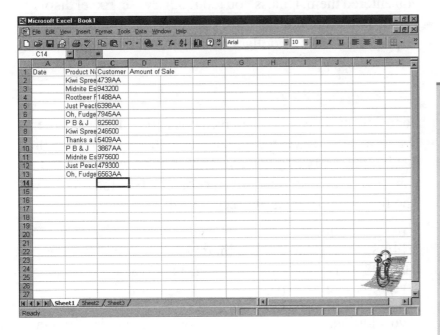

Entering Values

As you have seen, entering numeric values is just as easy as entering text. Follow along with the next two steps as you enter the sales amounts in column D:

1. Click cell D2 to select the first cell in the Amount of Sale column, and type *1456.23*. Press Enter to complete the entry, which Excel right-aligns in its cell.

2. Type the following amounts in the indicated cells, pressing Enter after each one:

D3	*875.56*
D4	*2068.30*
D5	*1399.07*
D6	*2643.90*
D7	*10576.40*
D8	*345.23*
D9	*1168.34*
D10	*2256.23*
D11	*656.90*
D12	*345.00*
D13	*2531.76*

Long numeric values

Excel allows a long text entry to overflow into an adjacent empty cell and truncates the entry only if the adjacent cell also contains an entry. However, Excel treats a long numeric value differently. By default, ordinary values are displayed in scientific notation, and values with many decimal places might be rounded. As an example, if you were to enter 12345678912345 in a standard width cell (a standard width cell holds 8.43 characters), Excel displays 1.23457E+13 (1.23457 times 10 to the 13th power). And if you enter 123456.789 in a standard width cell, Excel displays 123456.8. In both cases, Excel leaves the underlying value unchanged. You can widen the column to display the decimal value in the format in which you entered it, but in the default General format, values with more than 10 digits are always displayed in scientific notation. If you enter a large value in a standard-width cell, Excel automatically adjusts the width of the column to accommodate the entry. If you manually set the width of a column and then enter a currency value that is too large to be displayed in its entirety, Excel displays pound signs (#) instead of the value. (Adjusting the width of columns is discussed on pages 19 and 45.)

Don't worry if Excel does not display these values exactly as you entered them. Unless you tell it otherwise, Excel displays values in their simplest form. On page 50, you tell Excel to display the values as dollars and cents, and then the missing zeros will reappear.

Entering Dates and Times

For a date or time to be displayed correctly, you must enter it in a format that Excel recognizes as a date or time. Excel then displays the entry as you want it but stores it as a value so that you can perform date and time arithmetic (see the tip below). The following formats are recognized:

3/14	14-Mar	Mar-98	M
3/14/98	14-Mar-98	March-98	M-98
03/14/98	14-Mar-98	March 14, 1998	
3/14/1998	14-Mar-1998		

Two additional formats combine both date and time and take these forms:

3/14/98 1:30 PM   3/14/98 13:30

Let's see how Excel handles different date formats:

1. Type the dates shown here in the indicated cells, pressing the Enter key after each one:

A2	*Jan 4, 1999*
A3	*1/8/99*
A4	*1/11/99*
A5	*25-Jan-99*
A6	*Feb 2, 99*
A7	*2/8/99*
A8	*feb 15, 99*
A9	*3/1/99*
A10	*11-March-99*
A11	*3-15-99*
A12	*3/22/99*
A13	*March 29, 1999*

Again, don't worry if Excel displays the dates differently from the way you entered them. Later, you'll come back and make sure all the dates appear in the same format. As you can

Date and time arithmetic

Each date you enter is internally recorded by Excel as a value representing the number of days that have elapsed between that date and the base date of January 1, 1900, which is assigned the value 1. As a result, you can perform arithmetic with dates—for example, you can have Excel determine whether a payment is past due. Similarly, when you enter a time, it is internally recorded as a decimal value that represents the portion of the day that has elapsed between that time and the base time of 12:00 midnight.

see here, you've now completed all the columns of this simple worksheet:

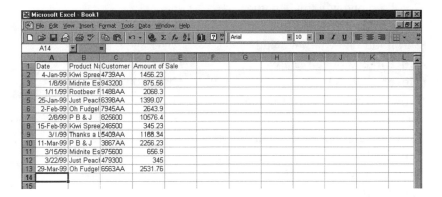

Moving Around

The fastest way to move around the worksheet is with the mouse. As you've seen, clicking any cell moves the cell pointer to that location and displays a new reference in the name box at the left end of the formula bar. To display parts of the worksheet that are currently out of sight, you can use the scroll bars, which function the same way as scroll bars in all Windows applications. Try this:

1. Select cell A1 and click the arrows at the bottom of the vertical scroll bar and the right end of the horizontal scroll bar until cell P37 comes into view.

   Using the scroll bars

2. Drag the scroll box in the vertical scroll bar. As you drag, Excel displays the number of the row that will appear at the top of the window when you release the mouse button. If you drag the horizontal scroll box, Excel displays the letter of the column that will appear at the left edge of the window.

3. Stop dragging, and then press Ctrl+Home to jump all the way back to cell A1.

   Jumping to cell A1

As we just demonstrated, you can use the keyboard to move around the worksheet. You'll probably use the four arrow keys most often, but as you gain more experience with Excel, you might find other keys and key combinations useful for moving around by more than one cell at a time. Turn the page to find a list of some of the navigation keys and what they do.

To do this...	Use this...
Scroll down one window length	Page Down
Scroll up one window length	Page Up
Scroll right one window width	Alt+Page Down
Scroll left one window width	Alt+Page Up
Move to end of active area	Ctrl+End
Move to cell A1	Ctrl+Home
Move to first cell in row containing active cell	Home
Move to last cell in row containing active cell	End, then Right Arrow
Move to first cell in column containing active cell	End, then Up Arrow
Move to last cell in column containing active cell	End, then Down Arrow

Selecting Ranges

Well, you've created a basic worksheet. But before we can show you some of the things you can do with it, we first need to discuss how to select blocks of cells, called *ranges*. Any rectangular block or blocks containing more than one cell is a range. A range can include two cells, an entire row or column, or the entire worksheet. *Range references* consist of the address of the cell in the top left corner of the rectangular block and the address of the cell in the bottom right corner, separated by a colon. For example, A1:B2 identifies the range that consists of cells A1, A2, B1, and B2.

Ranges ➝

Range references ➝

Selecting and working with ranges saves you time because you can apply formats to or reference the whole range, instead of dealing with each cell individually. To learn how to select ranges, follow the steps on the facing page.

Selecting more than one block

A range can consist of more than one block of cells. To select a multi-block range, select the first range, hold down the Ctrl key, select the next range, and so on.

The Go To command

Another way to move around the worksheet is with the Go To command. Choose Go To from the expanded Edit menu to display the Go To dialog box. Type the address of the cell you want to move to in the Reference edit box and click OK. Immediately, Excel scrolls the worksheet and selects that cell. The Go To list in the dialog box records the locations you have jumped to, so you can easily return to a cell you have previously visited by selecting it and clicking OK.

1. Point to cell A1, hold down the left mouse button, and drag diagonally to cell D13 without releasing the button. Notice as you drag that the reference in the name box at the left end of the formula bar reads 13R x 4C, which indicates that you are selecting a range of cells 13 rows high by 4 columns wide. Notice also that the selection's column and row *headers*—the gray boxes at the top of the columns containing letters and at the left end of the rows containing numbers—are now bold.

Selecting with the mouse

2. Release the mouse button when the range A1:D13 is highlighted. As you can see here, cell A1—the cell where you started the selection—is white, indicating that it is the active cell in the range:

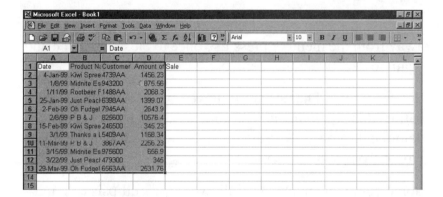

3. Press Ctrl+Home to move to cell A1, and then click column B's header—the gray box at the top of the column containing the letter *B*—to select the entire column. (You can select an entire row by clicking its header.)

Selecting entire columns and rows

Next try selecting ranges with the keyboard:

1. Select cell B6, hold down the Shift key, press the Right Arrow key twice and the Down Arrow key twice, and release the Shift key. The range B6:D8 is selected.

Selecting with the keyboard

2. Click anywhere on the worksheet to deselect the range.

Giving Excel Instructions

Now that you know how to select cells and ranges, let's cover how you tell Excel what it should do with the selection.

Using Menus

You can give Excel instructions by choosing *commands* that are arranged in *menus* on the *menu bar*. Because this basic procedure is the same for all Windows applications, we assume that you are familiar with it. Here's a quick review:

Choosing commands

- To choose a command from a menu, you first click the menu name on the menu bar. When the menu drops down, you simply click the name of the command you want.

- To choose a command with the keyboard, you press the Alt key to activate the menu bar, press the underlined letter of the name of the menu, then press the underlined letter of the command you want.

- To close a menu without choosing a command, you click away from the menu or press Esc once to close the menu and again to deactivate the menu bar.

Submenus

- Some command names are followed by an arrowhead, indicating that a *submenu* will appear when you choose that command. You choose commands from submenus as you would from regular menus.

Dialog boxes

- Some command names are followed by an ellipsis (...), indicating that you must supply more information before Excel can carry out the command. When you choose one of these commands, Excel displays a *dialog box*. Some dialog boxes have several sheets called *tabs*. You can display the options on a tab by clicking it. You give the information needed to carry out a command by typing in an *edit box* or by selecting options from *lists* and clicking *check boxes* and *option buttons*. You close the dialog box and carry out the command according to your specifications by clicking a *command button*— usually OK or Close—or by clicking the Close button in the top right corner. Clicking Cancel closes the dialog box and cancels the command. Other command buttons might be available to open other dialog boxes or to refine the original command.

- Some command names are occasionally displayed in gray letters, indicating that you can't choose them. For example,

Corresponding buttons

You may notice that some menu commands have an icon to the left of their names. This indicates that a corresponding button exists for this command on one of Excel's toolbars.

the Unhide command on the Window menu appears in gray until you have used the Hide command.

Excel 2000 goes beyond the basic Windows procedure for choosing commands by determining which commands you are most likely to use and adjusting the display of commands on each menu to reflect how you use the program. As a quick example, follow these steps to apply a display format to the dates you entered in column A of the worksheet:

1. Use the mouse or keyboard to select the range A2:A13, which contains the dates.

2. Click Format on the menu bar to drop down the Format menu. The two arrows at the bottom of the menu indicate that one or more commands are hidden because they are not the ones most people use most of the time.

Short menus

3. Continue pointing to the word *Format*. (You can also click the two arrows if you're impatient.) The two arrows disappear and the Style command appears on the menu, like this:

Expanded menus

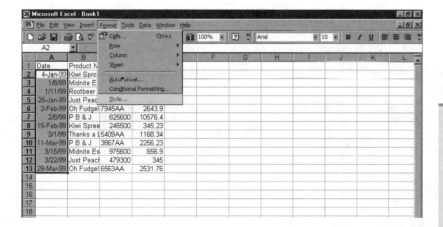

Notice that the Style command's status as a less frequently used command is indicated by a lighter shade of gray. If you choose this command, in the future it will appear in the same color as other commands and will no longer be hidden.

4. Click the Cells command to display the dialog box shown on the next page.

Using keyboard shortcuts

If you don't get along with your mouse and you prefer to use the keyboard, you can access many Excel commands with keyboard shortcuts. You can display lists of these shortcuts by opening the Help window, clicking the plus sign to the left of the *Using Short-cut Keys* category on the Contents tab, clicking *Keyboard shortcuts*, and then clicking the keyboard shortcut topic you're interested in. (For more about Excel's Help system, see page 24.)

The six tabs of the Format Cells dialog box provide you with all the options you need to format cells. The Number tab should be displayed. If it isn't, click it.

5. Click Date in the Category list, then click the various possibilities in the Type list, noticing in the Sample box how your dates will appear with the selected format. Select the first 14-Mar-98 option and click OK to close the dialog box and apply the format to the selected cells.

6. Press Ctrl+Home to move to cell A1. Excel displays all the dates in the same format, as shown here:

Help with dialog boxes

In the top right corner of most dialog boxes is a question mark button that provides information about the dialog box, including how to complete its edit boxes and select its options. To use the question mark button, click it once and then click an item in the dialog box. A pop-up window appears, containing information about the item.

Using Shortcut Menus

Shortcut menus are context-sensitive menus that group together the commands used frequently with a specific type of object, such as a cell or a window element. You display the shortcut menu by pointing to the object and clicking the right mouse button. (From now on, we refer to this action as *right-clicking*.) You can then choose a command from the menu in the usual way. Try this:

Right-clicking

1. Point to column B's header (the gray box containing the letter *B*), and right-click to select the entire column and to display this shortcut menu:

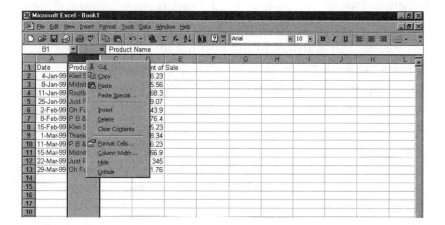

2. Choose Column Width from the menu to display this dialog box, where Excel has entered the column's current width:

Widening columns

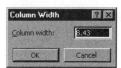

3. In the Column Width edit box, type *16* and press Enter (the equivalent of clicking OK). Excel almost doubles the width of the cells in the selected column, where all the entries are now completely visible.

4. Select columns C and D by pointing to C's header, holding down the left mouse button, dragging across D's header, and releasing the button. Then repeat steps 1 through 3 to widen these two columns simultaneously.

Selecting multiple columns

On page 45, we show you another way to adjust the width of a single column, but as you have seen, using a command on a shortcut menu is the most efficient way of adjusting more than one column. Here's another example:

1. Right-click the Office Assistant to display a shortcut menu of things you can do with Excel's helper.

2. Choose Hide from the shortcut menu to temporarily turn off the Office Assistant.

Using Toolbars

Another way to give an instruction is by clicking a button on a toolbar. This is the equivalent of choosing the corresponding command from a menu and if necessary, clicking OK to accept all the default settings in the command's dialog box. Excel comes with many built-in toolbars, equipped with buttons that help you accomplish specific tasks. You will use some toolbars frequently, and others you may never use. By default, Excel displays two of its most useful toolbars—the Standard and Formatting toolbars—on a single toolbar row below the menu bar. It overlaps the toolbars and, as with menus, initially displays only the most frequently used buttons on each bar. As shown here, each toolbar has a move handle at its left end and a More Buttons button at its right end, both of which allow you to display currently hidden buttons:

The More Buttons button

Standard toolbar | More Buttons button | Formatting toolbar

Move handle —

Move handle | More Buttons button |

Throughout this book we use toolbar buttons whenever possible because they are often the fastest way to access commands. Let's do some exploring:

ScreenTips

1. Point to any button on the Standard toolbar. Excel's *Screen-Tips* feature displays a box with the button's name.

2. Move the pointer slowly over each button on the Standard and Formatting toolbars so that ScreenTips displays its name.

The Bold button

3. Select A1:D1 and click the Bold button on the Formatting toolbar to display the column headings in bold type, like this:

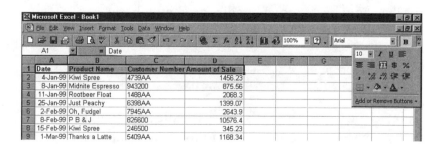

Notice that the Bold button now appears "pressed." If a selection is already bold, clicking the pressed Bold button turns off bold formatting. This type of button is called a *toggle*, because it toggles a specific feature on and off.

Suppose you want to display more buttons on the Standard toolbar and fewer buttons on the Formatting toolbar. Here's what you do:

1. Point to the Formatting toolbar's move handle. When the pointer changes to a four-headed arrow, drag it to the right as far as you can. Here are the results:

Formatting toolbar

Move handle   *More Buttons button*

2. Now click the Formatting toolbar's More Buttons button to see this palette of all the hidden buttons on that toolbar:

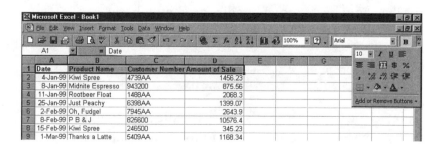

The Center button

3. With A1:D1 still selected, click the Center button. As well as centering the column headings in their selected cells, Excel

adjusts the relative amount of space allocated to the two tool-bars on the toolbar row so that it can display the Center button, as shown below:

You can display and hide any toolbar at any time. You can also move, resize, and hide the toolbars. Let's experiment with a different toolbar:

Displaying toolbars ─────▶ 1. Right-click anywhere on the Standard or Formatting toolbar to display a shortcut menu that lists other available toolbars, like this one:

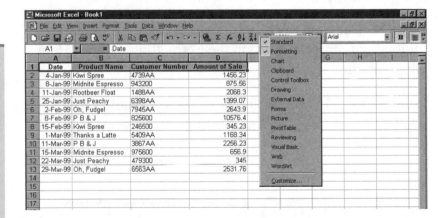

Personalized menus and toolbars

As you have seen, Excel's menus and toolbars adjust themselves to the way you work, making more commands and buttons available as you use them. Commands and buttons you don't use are hidden so that they don't get in the way. As a result, your menus and tool-bars may not look exactly like ours, and occasionally we may tell you to choose a command or click a button that is not visible. When this happens, don't panic. Simply pull down the menu and wait for all its commands to be displayed, or click the toolbar's More Buttons button to display its hidden buttons. To change the way the personalized menus and toolbars work, choose Toolbars and then Customize from the View menu. Then click the Op-tions tab, select or deselect the options you want to change, and click Close.

2. Choose Chart from the shortcut menu to display a floating Chart toolbar with a title bar and a Close button.

3. Double-click the toolbar's title bar to "dock" it above the worksheet. The toolbar's title bar disappears and the docked toolbar now has a move handle, as shown here:

4. Point to the Chart toolbar's move handle and drag the toolbar up into the toolbar row so that it joins the overlapped Standard and Formatting toolbars.

5. Drag the Chart toolbar from the toolbar row over the work-sheet, where it becomes a floating toolbar once again.

6. Drag the floating toolbar by its title bar all the way to the right. When you think it is going to disappear off the screen, the toolbar changes shape and docks itself along the right edge.

7. Experiment with moving the Chart toolbar to various positions, and docking and undocking it. (Notice that double-clicking the floating toolbar's title bar docks the toolbar wherever it was last docked.)

8. Finally, either click the Close button at the right end of the toolbar's title bar or right-click a toolbar and choose Chart from the shortcut menu to remove the toolbar from the screen.

Hiding toolbars

Saving Workbooks

Let's save the workbook you are working with for future use. As you'll see if you follow these steps, the first time you save a workbook, you must give its file a name:

1. Click the Save button on the Standard toolbar. Because you have not yet assigned a name to the workbook, Excel displays the Save As dialog box shown here:

The Save button

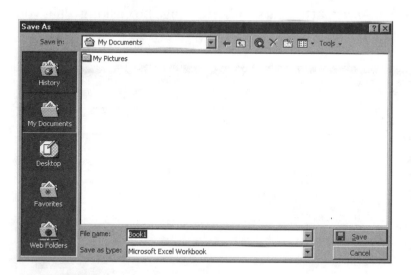

2. Excel suggests Book1 as the name for the first workbook created in this session. This name is not very descriptive, so with Book1 highlighted in the File Name edit box, type *1999 Sales*.

3. Be sure the My Documents folder appears in the Save In box and, leaving the other settings in the dialog box as they are,

Saving in another folder

To store a file in a folder different from the one designated in the Save In box, click the arrow to the right of the Save In box, then use the drop-down list to find the folder you want. Double-click that folder to display its name in the Save In box, and then click Save. You can also use the icons on the shortcuts bar along the left side of the Save As dialog box to quickly navigate to common folders and recent files. To make a new folder, click the Create New Folder button and name the folder before you save the file. To change the default folder from My Documents, choose Options from Excel's Tools menu, and in the File Location edit box on the General tab, enter a different folder name or path.

click Save. When you return to the worksheet, notice that the name 1999 Sales has replaced Book1 in the title bar.

Saving existing workbooks

From now on, you can save this workbook by simply clicking the Save button. Excel then saves the workbook by overwriting the previous version with a new version. If you want to save the changes you have made to a workbook but preserve the previous version, you can assign the new version a different name by choosing the Save As command from the File menu, entering a new filename, and clicking Save.

Getting Help

Are you worried that you might not remember everything we've covered so far? Don't be. If you forget how to carry out a particular task, help is never far away. You have already seen how the ScreenTips feature can jog your memory about the functions of the toolbar buttons. Here we'll take a look at ways to get information using the Office Assistant. Follow these steps:

1. Choose Microsoft Excel Help from the Help menu. The Office Assistant appears with a message box asking what you would like to do:

Saving options

To save an Excel workbook in a different format, click the arrow to the right of the Save As Type edit box and then select the desired format. (Formats available include text only, previous versions of Excel and other spreadsheet programs, and web page.) Clicking the Tools button and choosing General Options displays the Save Options dialog box. Selecting Always Create Backup tells Excel to create a copy of the existing workbook before overwriting it with the new version. Excel gives the copy the name Backup of *Filename*. If you assign a password in the Password To Open edit box, Excel won't open the workbook until the password is entered correctly. If you assign a password in the Password To Modify edit box, Excel opens a read-only version of the workbook if no password is entered. Selecting Read-Only Recommended tells Excel to warn users that the workbook should be opened as read-only, but does not prevent opening the workbook in the usual way.

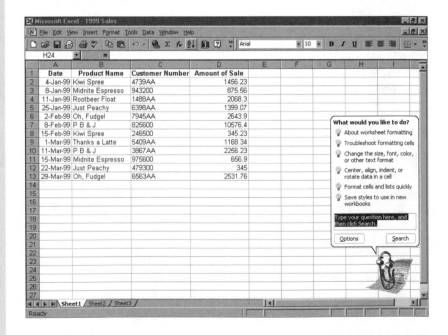

2. Type *Turn you off* in the Search box and then click the Search
   button to have the Office Assistant search for topics that most
   closely match what you want to do. The Office Assistant displays another message box:

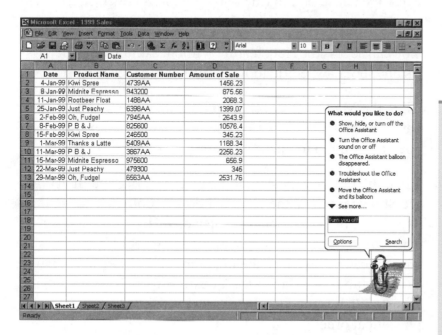

3. Click the *Show, hide, or turn off the Office Assistant* option
   to display a Help window with the requested information, as
   shown below:

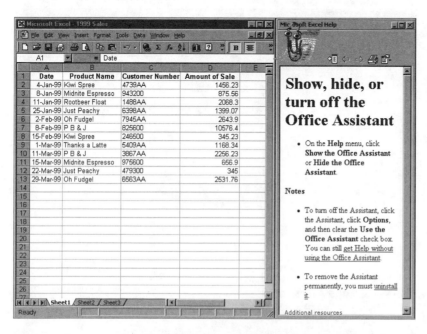

More about the Office Assistant

If the Office Assistant displays a light bulb above its icon, it has a tip for you. Click the light bulb to see the tip. To move the Office Assistant to another location on the screen, you can simply drag it. To display the search box, click the Office Assistant. If having the Office Assistant on the screen bothers you, or if you would like to customize it, click the Office Assistant's Options button to open the Office Assistant dialog box. Here, you can select and deselect various options that control when the Office Assistant appears, whether it makes sounds, and what tips it displays. To turn off the Office Assistant, deselect the Use The Office Assistant check box. (If you want the Office Assistant to temporarily disappear or reappear, choose Hide/Show The Office Assistant from the Help menu.) On the Gallery tab, you can click the Back and Next buttons to scroll through the different animated characters for the assistant (the default is the paper clip) and then click OK to change the assistant. (To complete the switch you may need to insert your installation CD-ROM.)

4. Without closing the Microsoft Excel Help window, click other options in the Office Assistant's message box to display their topics in the Help window.

5. Click the Close button (the one with the X) to close the Help window.

You can access the Help feature without asking the Office Assistant about a specific topic by following these steps:

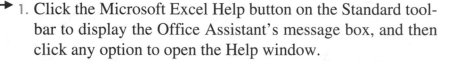

The Microsoft Excel Help button

1. Click the Microsoft Excel Help button on the Standard toolbar to display the Office Assistant's message box, and then click any option to open the Help window.

The Show button

2. Click the Office Assistant to turn off its box, and then click the Show button on the Help window's toolbar. The window expands to include Contents, Answer Wizard, and Index tabs. The Contents tab organizes all of the Excel Help topics in subject categories, like the chapters of a book; the Answer Wizard tab is similar to the question format of the Office Assistant's box, and the Index tab lists topic keywords in alphabetical order.

Using the Help Index

3. If necessary, drag the Office Assistant out of the way, and then click the Index tab to display this window:

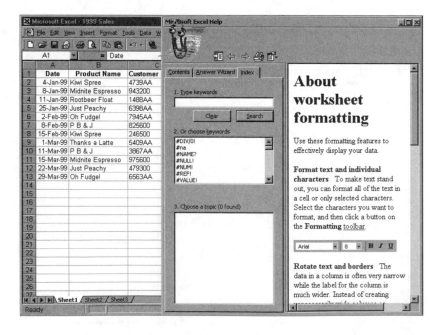

4. In the Type Keywords edit box, type *assistant*. The topic list in the box below scrolls to display the closest match to your keyword.

5. Click the Search button. The Choose A Topic box now displays all the topics that have anything even remotely to do with your keyword.

6. Click the *Show, hide, or turn off the Office Assistant* topic to display the Help information shown on page 25.

7. Move the pointer over *get Help without using the Office Assistant*, which is blue and underlined to indicate that clicking it will take you to another help topic. When the pointer changes to a hand, click the left mouse button.

8. Read through the instructions and then close the window.

We'll leave you to explore other Help topics on your own.

Quitting Excel

Well, that's it for the basic tour. All that's left is to show you how to end an Excel session. Follow these steps:

1. Click the Close button at the right end of Excel's title bar.

2. If the Office Assistant asks whether you want to save the changes you have made to the open worksheet, click Yes. After Excel closes, the Office Assistant leaves the screen.

Here are some other ways to quit Excel:

- Choose Exit from the File menu.

- Press Alt, then F, and then X.

- Double-click the Control menu icon—the X next to the words *Microsoft Excel*—at the left end of Excel's title bar.

Other ways of using help

The Contents tab of the Help window displays various main topics which you can choose by clicking the plus sign to the left of the topic. (A book icon indicates that the topic includes subtopics.) Help then displays a list of subtopics which you can choose in the same way. When you click an actual Help topic (indicated by the question mark icon), Help displays the information in the right pane. The Answer Wizard tab of the Help window provides a way to type questions without the Office Assistant interface. Simply type a question in the edit box and click Search. You then see a list of topics that most closely fit your question. You can double-click one of the topics to display its contents in the pane on the right. If you have a modem and are connected to the Internet, you can quickly access Microsoft's Web site to get help or technical support. Choose Office On The Web from the Help menu to start Internet Explorer, connect to the Internet, and display a page at Microsoft's Web site.

2

Editing and Formatting Worksheets

In this chapter, we show you how to edit worksheets and check spelling. You then learn some handy techniques for editing workbooks. Next we cover some formatting basics, and finally, we complete the chapter with a brief discussion of templates.

The techniques we describe here apply to any worksheet you might want to create to store tabular information.

Worksheets created and concepts covered:

Apply formatting to multiple worksheets simultaneously

Group worksheets so that the work you do in one is applied to the entire group

Dress up titles and subtitles by varying the font and size

Copy formatting with a couple of clicks

Wrap cell entries to multiple lines so that columns can be narrower

Check the spelling of text entries

Insert entire columns or rows

Use a currency format to display values as dollars and cents

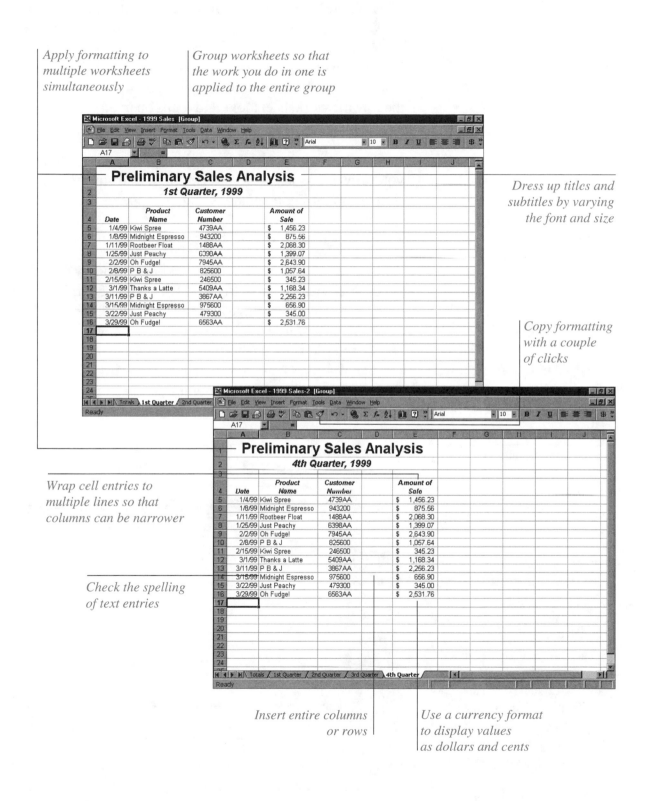

There are many tasks you might want to perform with a worksheet, and as long as the worksheet is accurate, it will do its job well enough. Your first priority is making sure that the worksheet is set up properly. When the content of the worksheet is correct, you can turn your attention to the way the worksheet looks and focus on making its information easy to decipher.

In this chapter, we cover the editing techniques that enable you to produce accurate information, and then we look at simple formatting techniques that enhance its readability.

Opening Existing Workbooks

When you first start Excel, the workbook window contains a blank document named Book1. There are several ways to open a workbook you have already created. If the workbook is one of the last four you have worked with, you can simply choose the file from the bottom of the File menu. Otherwise, you can use the Open button on the Standard toolbar or the Open command on the File menu to retrieve the workbook. Follow these steps to use the button method:

The Open button

1. If necessary, start Excel, and then click the Open button on the Standard toolbar to display this dialog box:

File management

Instead of having to manage files in Windows Explorer or My Computer, you can delete, rename, or move your files in Excel's Open or Save As dialog box. For example, you can right-click a filename in the Open dialog box and choose a shortcut menu command that allows you to print the file, send a copy of it to a floppy disk, e-mail a copy of it, delete it, or rename it.

2. Excel should display the contents of your My Documents folder (the folder displayed when you last saved or opened

a workbook). If it doesn't, click the My Documents icon on the shortcuts bar to display the contents of the My Documents folder on your hard drive.

3. If 1999 Sales is already selected, click the Open button to open the workbook. If it is not already selected, double-click it to simultaneously select and open it.

Editing Basics

While creating the 1999 Sales workbook in Chapter 1, you may have corrected the odd typo or two by backspacing over errors and retyping entries correctly. You can take care of most simple edits this way. But for more complicated changes, you can use a variety of more sophisticated editing techniques, as you'll see when you follow the examples in this section.

Changing Entries

First let's cover how to change individual entries. Glancing at the Amount of Sale column in Sheet1 of the 1999 Sales workbook, notice that the amount in cell D7 is suspiciously large compared with all the other amounts. Suppose you check this number and find to your disappointment that the amount should be 1057.64, not 10576.4. To correct the entry without having to retype the whole thing, follow these steps:

1. Double-click cell D7 to select the cell and position an insertion point in the entry. (You can also click the cell and press F2.)

2. Point between the 7 and 6 in the cell and click the left mouse button to reposition the insertion point. Then type a period.

3. Click between the second period and the 4 and press the Backspace key to delete the second period.

4. Press Enter to confirm the corrected entry.

Copying Entries

You can copy an entry or group of entries anywhere within the same worksheet or in a different worksheet. Copy operations involve the use of two buttons: Copy and Paste. You can click

Finding workbooks

You can easily search for and locate files while in the Open dialog box. Suppose you can't remember exactly what you called the 1999 Sales workbook or where you stored it. Simply click the Tools button and click Find. Next select the appropriate drive in the Look In drop-down list, click the Search Subfolders check box to look in all subfolders of the selected drive, and check that File Name is displayed in the Property edit box. Select the appropriate option in the Condition edit box and then enter *Sales* in the Value edit box. To begin the search, click Add To List to add your criteria to the criteria list, and then click Find Now. Excel searches the specified drive and its subfolders for any workbooks with the word *Sales* in the filename and displays the one(s) it finds. You can then select the workbook you want and click the Open button. If you have many files with similar names, you can refine the search by specifying other properties such as text included in the workbook or its date of modification. To save a search, click the Save Search button, name the search, and click OK.

these buttons on the Standard toolbar, or you can choose the equivalent commands from the Edit menu. Follow these steps:

The Copy button

1. Select A1:D13 and click the Copy button or choose Copy from the Edit menu. Excel surrounds the selection with a moving dotted line and stores a copy of the entries in the selected range on the *Clipboard* (see the tip below).

The Paste button

2. Select cell E1 and click the Paste button or choose Paste from the Edit menu. Excel assumes that the selected cell is the top left corner of the paste area and pastes the copied entries into E1:H13. Notice that you don't have to select the entire paste area. Also notice that Excel does not transfer the column-width settings of the copied cells to the paste area.

Now try using Excel's shortcut menus:

1. First select cell F1 and then right-click to display the shortcut menu shown below. (We've turned off the Office Assistant. See the tip on page 25 if you want to do the same.)

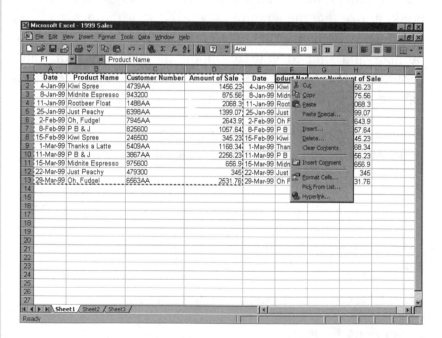

2. Choose Paste from the shortcut menu. Excel uses the selected cell as the top left corner of the paste area and, without warning, pastes the copied cells over the existing contents of cells F1:I13, as shown on the facing page.

The Office Clipboard

In Excel, you have access to two clipboards. The Windows Clipboard stores only your most recent cut or copied item. The Office Clipboard stores up to 12 items. If you want to cut or copy several items from one or more workbooks and paste them elsewhere, you can do so easily. After selecting one item and then clicking the Cut or Copy button, cutting or copying another item displays the Clipboard toolbar, where each item is represented by the icon of the program in which it was created. (The Office Clipboard stores items from any Windows application.) Point to an icon to have ScreenTips display its contents. To paste an item, simply click an insertion point and then click the icon that represents the item you want to paste. To paste all of the items at once, click the Paste All button on the Clipboard toolbar. To clear items from the Office Clipboard, click the Clear Clipboard button. To turn off the Clipboard toolbar, simply click its Close button.

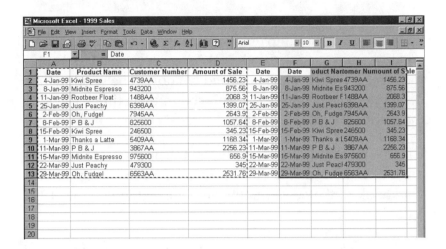

Cause for panic? Not at all. Excel's Undo command is designed for just such an occasion.

The Undo button

3. Click the Undo button or choose Undo Paste from the Edit menu. Excel restores your worksheet to its prepaste status.

Up to now, you have been working with Sheet1 of the 1999 Sales workbook, but suppose you need to set up a second worksheet with a structure similar to that of Sheet1. Do you have to enter all the information again? No; you can copy between worksheets, or even between workbooks, as easily as within one worksheet. The information you just copied is still on the Clipboard, so let's put a copy of it in Sheet2:

1. Click the Sheet2 tab to display that sheet.

2. With cell A1 selected, click the Paste button. Excel faithfully pastes in a copy of the range from Sheet1.

3. Click the Sheet1 tab, press Ctrl+Home to return to cell A1, and press Esc to remove the selection marquee.

Moving Entries

The procedure for moving cell entries is almost identical to that for copying entries. Again, you use two buttons: Cut and Paste. You can click these buttons on the Standard toolbar, or you can choose the equivalent commands from the Edit menu. In the following example, you'll move entries from one worksheet to another worksheet in the same workbook. When

Undoing and redoing multiple actions

You can undo and redo several actions at once. Simply click the arrow to the right of the appropriate button to drop down a list of actions, with the latest at the top. Then drag through the actions in the list that you want to undo or redo. You cannot undo or redo a single action other than the latest one you performed. For example, to undo the third action in the list, you must also undo the first and second actions.

working with two different worksheets in the same workbook, it is sometimes easier to display each worksheet in a separate window. You can use the New Window command to display the current workbook in a second window. The windows are distinguished by numbers displayed in their title bars, after the workbook name. Try this:

Displaying a second window

1. Click Window on the menu bar and then choose New Window from the expanded menu. Excel displays a copy of the workbook in the new window and names the window 1999 Sales:2.

2. Click Window on the menu bar to drop down its menu, and notice that the names of the two windows appear at the bottom of the menu. Click 1999 Sales:1 to display it.

Arranging windows

3. To view both windows on the screen at the same time, choose Arrange from the expanded Window menu to display this dialog box:

Other window arrangements

In addition to the Tiled option, which arranges windows like tiles on a counter, the Arrange Windows dialog box offers three other configurations. Selecting the Horizontal option allocates an equal amount of horizontal screen space to each open window; selecting Vertical allocates an equal amount of vertical space. Selecting Cascade arranges the windows so that they overlap in a fan, with the title bar of each of them visible. If you have more than one workbook open, you can arrange only the windows in which the current workbook is displayed by selecting the Windows Of Active Workbook check box.

4. Click OK to accept the default Tiled option. Your window now looks like this:

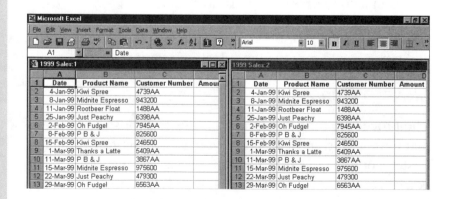

5. In 1999 Sales:1, scroll columns E through H into view and select E1:H13.

6. Click the Standard toolbar's More Buttons button and then click the Cut button.

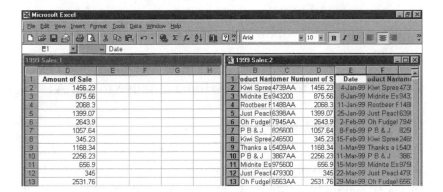

The Cut button

7. Activate 1999 Sales:2 by clicking its title bar and then click that window's Sheet2 tab.

8. Select cell E1 in Sheet2 and click the Paste button. Excel moves the entries from Sheet1 of 1999 Sales:1 to Sheet2 of 1999 Sales:2. The worksheets now look like this:

You can also move entries by dragging them with the mouse and "dropping" them in their new location. Here's how *drag-and-drop editing* works:

Drag-and-drop editing

1. Point to the bottom border of the selected range in Sheet2. When the pointer changes to a hollow arrow, hold down the Alt key and the left mouse button and drag the outline of the selection to the Sheet3 tab (don't release the key or the mouse button yet). Sheet3 opens.

2. While still holding down the left mouse button and the Alt key, drag the outline of the selection over the range A1:D13. Then release the mouse button and the Alt key. Excel moves the selected entries from Sheet2 to their new location in Sheet3.

3. Now display the Sheet3 tab of 1999 Sales:1, which contains the same information as Sheet3 of 1999 Sales:2 because the same workbook is open in both windows. (Later in this chapter, you will work with different workbooks open in two windows; see page 42.)

Copying and moving with the keyboard

You can use keyboard shortcuts to copy a range and then paste it into your worksheet. Select the range and press Ctrl+C. Then click the cell in the top left corner of the destination range and press Ctrl+V. To move the range instead of copying it, follow the same procedure but use Ctrl+X instead of Ctrl+C.

You can also copy rather than move entries between worksheets using drag-and-drop editing. Just hold down Ctrl+Alt and the left mouse button while dragging.

Now that you're finished moving data between sheets, you can close the second window:

1. Close the 1999 Sales:2 window by first clicking its title bar to activate it and then clicking its Close button.

Maximizing windows → 2. Maximize the 1999 Sales window by clicking its Maximize button—the middle of the three buttons at the right end of the title bar.

3. Display Sheet1 and press Ctrl+Home to move to cell A1.

Inserting and Deleting Cells

It is a rare person who can create a worksheet from scratch without ever having to tinker with its design—moving this block of data, changing that heading, or adding or deleting a column here and there. In this section, we'll show you how to insert and delete cells. Follow these steps:

Inserting columns → 1. Click the column D header—the box containing the letter *D*—to select the entire column.

2. Right-click the column and choose Insert from the shortcut menu. Excel inserts an entire blank column in front of the Amount of Sale column, which is now column E:

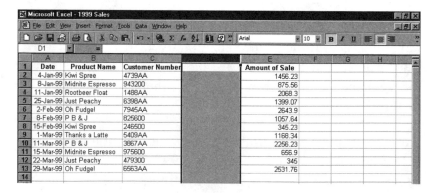

Inserting rows → Inserting a row works exactly the same way as inserting a column. You simply click the row header—the box containing the row number—to select the entire row and choose Insert from the row's shortcut menu.

What if you need to insert only a few cells and inserting an entire column or row will mess up some of your entries? You can insert cells anywhere you need them, as you'll see when you follow these steps:

1. Select E1:E10—all but three of the cells containing entries in column E—and choose Cells from the expanded Insert menu. Excel displays the dialog box shown here:

Inserting cells

Because you have selected a range rather than an entire column or row, Excel needs to know how to move the existing cells to make room for the inserted cells.

2. Click OK to accept the default option of shifting cells to the right. Excel inserts a new blank cell to the left of each selected cell, as shown here:

	A	B	C	D	E	F	G	H
1	Date	Product Name	Customer Number			Amount of Sale		
2	4-Jan-99	Kiwi Spree	4739AA			1456.23		
3	8-Jan-99	Midnite Espresso	943200			875.56		
4	11-Jan-99	Rootbeer Float	1488AA			2068.3		
5	25-Jan-99	Just Peachy	6398AA			1399.07		
6	2-Feb-99	Oh Fudge!	7945AA			2643.9		
7	8-Feb-99	P B & J	825600			1057.64		
8	15-Feb-99	Kiwi Spree	246500			345.23		
9	1-Mar-99	Thanks a Latte	5409AA			1168.34		
10	11-Mar-99	P B & J	3867AA			2256.23		
11	15-Mar-99	Midnite Espresso	975600		656.9			
12	22-Mar-99	Just Peachy	479300		345			
13	29-Mar-99	Oh Fudge!	6563AA		2531.76			
14								

You could undo this insertion to restore the integrity of the Amount of Sale column, but instead let's delete E1:E10:

1. With E1:E10 selected, right-click the selection and choose Delete from the shortcut menu. Excel displays a Delete dialog box similar to the Insert dialog box shown above.

Deleting cells

2. Click OK to accept the default option of shifting cells to the left to fill the gap created by the deleted cells. Excel deletes the cells, and the sale amounts are now back in one column.

Leave the empty column D where it is for now—you'll use it when you work with the 1999 Sales workbook again in the next chapter.

Clearing Cells

Clearing cells is different from cutting entries. Cutting entries assumes that you will paste the entries somewhere else, whereas clearing cells simply erases the entries. In the following example, you'll clear some cells on Sheet3 and Sheet2:

1. Click the Sheet3 tab and select A1:D13.

2. Choose Clear from the Edit menu. Excel displays the submenu shown here:

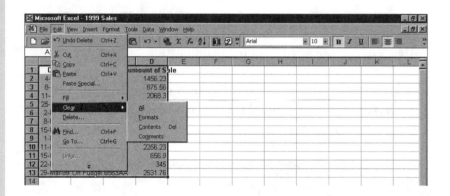

The All option clears all formats, contents, and comments from the cells. Formats clears only the formats, and Contents clears only the contents. Comments clears any attached comments (see the tip on page 43), leaving the formats and contents intact.

3. Choose All. The entries in the range disappear.

4. Display Sheet2, select A1:D13, and clear it by pressing the Delete key. Excel clears the contents of the cells. (When you press the Delete key, Excel leaves any formats and comments intact.)

5. Return to Sheet1 by clicking the Sheet1 tab.

AutoCorrect

Excel's AutoCorrect feature corrects simple typos as you enter text in a worksheet. For example, if you type *teh*, AutoCorrect automatically replaces it with *the*. By default, AutoCorrect also corrects two initial capital letters, corrects any sentences that don't begin with a capital letter, capitalizes the names of days, and corrects accidental usage of the Caps Lock key. You can turn off an option by choosing the AutoCorrect command from the Tools menu and when the AutoCorrect dialog box appears, deselecting the appropriate check box. To include your own commonly misspelled entries in AutoCorrect, type the misspelling in the Replace edit box and the correct spelling in the With edit box. Then click Add to add the new entry to AutoCorrect's list of common misspellings. (You might want to peruse this list to get a feel for the kinds of words AutoCorrect fixes by default.) You can also delete any entries in AutoCorrect's list by selecting the entry and clicking the Delete button. To turn the AutoCorrect feature off, deselect the Replace Text As You Type check box in the Auto-Correct dialog box.

Checking Spelling

An important part of ensuring a worksheet's accuracy is checking your spelling, so we'll pause here to discuss Excel's spell checker. You can check all or part of a worksheet for misspelled words and duplicate words within a block. From the Spelling dialog box, you can add words to one of the dictionaries Excel uses (see the tip below). Let's run a spell check:

1. Press Ctrl+Home to move to cell A1. Then move the Formatting toolbar to the right to display more Standard toolbar buttons.

2. Click the Spelling button. Excel starts checking the worksheet, stops on *Midnite*, and displays this dialog box:

The Spelling button

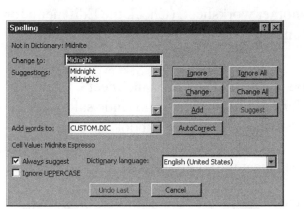

Excel suggests possible replacements for the misspelled word in the Suggestions list box and highlights the most likely candidate in the Change To edit box.

3. The suggestion, *Midnight*, is correct, so click the Change All button. The spell checker replaces both instances of the misspelled word and continues checking the worksheet.

4. Complete the spell check, clicking the Ignore or Ignore All button for any other words that Excel stumbles over.

5. When Excel finishes checking the worksheet, it displays a message box. Click OK to return to the worksheet.

Editing Workbooks

Up to now you have been making changes to the information on the worksheets in one workbook. Excel also allows you to

Excel's dictionaries

Excel checks your spelling by comparing each word in a worksheet to those in its built-in dictionary and in a supplemental dictionary called Custom.dic. If a word is not in either dictionary, Excel displays the Spelling dialog box and awaits your instructions. You can't edit the built-in dictionary, but you can add words to Custom.dic by clicking the Add button in the Spelling dialog box. To use special-purpose dictionaries, create a text-only file with each word you want to include on a separate line, and save the file in the C:\Windows\Application Data\Microsoft\Proof folder with the extension *dic*. Then when you start a spell check for which you want to use the special dictionary, select that dictionary from the Add Words To list when the Spelling dialog box appears.

move and copy entire worksheets, both within the same workbook and between different workbooks, as you'll see in the following examples.

Inserting and Deleting Worksheets

Suppose you want to insert a worksheet between Sheet1 and Sheet2. Here are the steps:

1. Click Sheet2's tab to make Sheet2 the active worksheet.

Inserting sheets

2. Choose Worksheet from the Insert menu. Excel inserts a new worksheet called Sheet4 to the left of the active sheet.

3. Choose Repeat Insert Worksheet from the expanded Edit menu to insert another worksheet. (Check the Edit menu for a Repeat command whenever you want to repeat your previous task.)

Now suppose you want to delete the blank Sheet3. Excel will delete the sheet permanently—there is no Undo safety net. So before you delete a sheet from a workbook, you should always do a quick visual confirmation to verify that you are sending the correct sheet into oblivion. Let's go:

1. Click Sheet3's tab to display that worksheet (it should be blank).

Deleting sheets

2. Choose Delete Sheet from the expanded Edit menu. Excel warns you that the sheet will be permanently deleted.

3. Click OK in the message box to remove Sheet3 from the 1999 Sales workbook.

Copying Worksheets

The procedure for copying information between worksheets in different workbooks is the same as for copying between worksheets in one workbook (see page 31). You can also copy entire sheets both within a workbook and between workbooks. Let's make a few copies of Sheet1:

1. Activate Sheet1 in 1999 Sales.

Changing the default number of worksheets

If you often create workbooks with more than three sheets, you can change this default number. Choose Options from the Tools menu and, on the General tab, increase the Sheets In New Workbook setting.

2. Point to the Sheet1 tab, hold down the left mouse button, and then hold down the Ctrl key. The pointer changes to an arrow with a sheet icon containing a plus sign attached to it.

3. Drag the sheet pointer until it sits to the right of Sheet2. (Excel indicates with an arrowhead where it will place the copy.) Release the mouse button and then the Ctrl key. Word makes a copy of Sheet1 called Sheet1 (2).

4. Repeat steps 2 and 3 to copy Sheet1 two more times, and then click the First Sheet button. Your screen now looks like this:

The First Sheet button

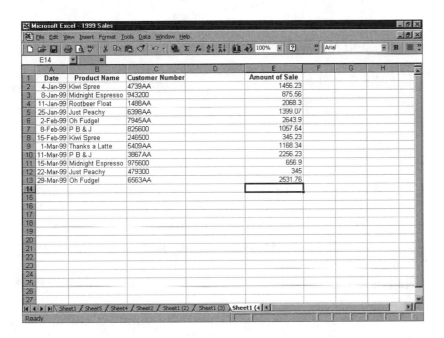

Naming Sheets

As you can see, when you insert, delete, and copy worksheets, Excel does not renumber the sheet tabs, so the tabs are no longer in logical sequence. You can change the names of the sheets to put them back in the correct numerical order, but if you're going to go to all that effort, it makes sense to change the names to something a little more meaningful than Sheet1, Sheet2, and so on. Here's how to rename the sheets:

1. Double-click the Sheet1 tab to select the text on the tab.

2. Type *1st Quarter* and press Enter. Excel displays the new name on the sheet tab.

3. Repeat steps 1 and 2 to rename Sheet1 (2) as *2nd Quarter*, Sheet1 (3) as *3rd Quarter*, and Sheet1 (4) as *4th Quarter*.

Moving Worksheets

You have already seen how you can effectively "move" a worksheet by moving all its information, but you can also literally move worksheets from one position in a workbook to another. Try this:

1. Activate the 1st Quarter worksheet, point to its tab, and hold down the left mouse button.

2. Drag the sheet pointer until it sits between Sheet2 and 2nd Quarter and release the mouse button.

3. Click the Save button to save your work.

You can also easily move a worksheet from one workbook to another. To complete this task, you must first open a new workbook:

The New button

1. Click the New button or choose New from the File menu. Excel displays a new workbook, called Book2.

2. To see both workbooks at the same time, choose Arrange from the Window menu and click OK to accept the default Tiled option.

3. In 1999 Sales, rename Sheet5 as *Trial Balance*, Sheet4 as *Gross Income*, and Sheet2 as *Totals*.

Now you'll move the Trial Balance and Gross Income sheets to Book2:

1. First activate the Trial Balance worksheet, and then drag the sheet pointer until it sits to the left of Sheet1 in the Book2 workbook.

2. Repeat step 1 to move the Gross Income sheet between Trial Balance and Sheet1 of Book2. Your screen now looks like the one shown at the top of the facing page.

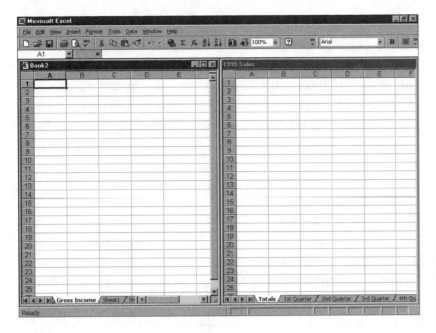

You don't need Book2 anymore, so let's close it without saving it:

1. Because Book2 is the active workbook, it has a set of buttons at the right end of its title bar. Click the Close button.

2. When the asked whether you want to save the changes to Book2, click No.

3. Maximize the 1999 Sales window and save the workbook.

Formatting Basics

Excel offers a variety of formatting options you can use to emphasize parts of a worksheet and display data in different ways. Here you'll use some of the common formatting options that are available on the Formatting toolbar and some of the options that are available in the Format Cells dialog box. You'll also learn a quick way to adjust the column widths. Because you will often want to work with sets of worksheets, like the quarterly worksheets in the 1999 Sales workbook, we'll take this opportunity to show you how to work with more than one worksheet at a time.

Attaching comments to cells

You might want to attach a comment to a cell for a variety of reasons (to explain a formula or remind yourself to check an assumption, for example). Simply select the cell, choose Comment from the Insert menu, and then type the comment in the text box that appears. (The comment is "signed" with the name entered when Excel was installed on your computer. You can edit or delete this signature.) Click anywhere outside the cell and text box to attach the comment. Excel places a red marker in the top right corner of any cell with a comment attached. To see a comment, just point to the cell. To permanently display the comment, right-click the cell and choose Show Comment from the shortcut menu. To edit or delete a comment, right-click the cell and choose either Edit Comment or Delete Comment from the shortcut menu. (You can also remove comments attached to a selected cell by choosing Clear and then Comments from the Edit menu.)

Changing Character Formatting

Just as you can use headings to make tables of data easier to read, you can use character formatting to distinguish different categories of information. This type of formatting changes the appearance of the worksheet's characters. For example, in the 1st Quarter worksheet you have already applied the Bold style to the column headings—you could also apply a color or add the Italic style. Because these character styles are used so often, Excel provides buttons for them. Try this:

Activating a group of worksheets

1. First activate the 1st Quarter worksheet, and then hold down the Shift key and click the tabs of each of the other quarterly worksheets to activate them as well. Excel adds the word *Group* in parenthesis after the workbook name in the title bar to indicate that a group of worksheets is active. Now any changes you make to the 1st Quarter worksheet will also be reflected in the other three sheets.

2. Select A1:E1, the range that contains the headings.

The Italic button

3. Click the Italic button. The headings are now displayed in both bold and italic.

Changing Alignment

As you know, by default Excel left-aligns text and right-aligns values. In Chapter 1, you overrode this default alignment for the column headings by using the Center button. Now try this:

The Align Left and Align Right buttons

1. Select column C and click the Align Left button and then the Align Right button, noting the effects.

2. When you're ready, click the Center button to center all the entries in the column.

3. In turn, click the 2nd Quarter, 3rd Quarter, and 4th Quarter tabs to verify that the formatting you have applied to the 1st Quarter worksheet has also been applied to the other active sheets.

4. Return to the 1st Quarter sheet.

Changing Column Widths

In Chapter 1, you widened the columns of the 1999 Sales worksheet by selecting columns, choosing Column Width from the shortcut menu, and setting a width in the resulting dialog box. Adjusting column widths this way can involve some trial and error. In this section, you'll look at other methods that dispense with the guesswork. First let's restore the original column widths:

1. Click the header for column A to select the column. Then point to the header for column E, hold down the Shift key, and click the header. Excel selects columns A through E.

2. Choose Column and then Width from the Format menu to display the dialog box shown earlier on page 19.

3. Type *8.43* in the Column Width edit box and press Enter to return to the worksheet with the selected columns set to the standard width.

Now let's fine-tune the width of the columns:

1. Press Ctrl+Home to move to cell A1.

2. Point to the line between the headers of columns B and C, hold down the left mouse button, drag to the right until column B is wide enough to display all of its entries, and then release the mouse button. (As you drag, Excel displays the width of the column in a pop-up box above the mouse pointer.)

Manual adjustment

3. Change the width of column C using the same method.

Follow the steps on the next page to widen column E using a different method.

Changing the standard width

You can change Excel's standard column width of 8.43 characters by choosing Column and then Standard Width from the Format menu, typing a new value in the Standard Width dialog box, and then clicking OK. (Note that columns whose widths you have already adjusted retain their custom widths.)

Column width shortcut

You can quickly adjust the width of a column to fit its longest entry by simply pointing to the right border of the column's header and then double-clicking.

1. Click column E's header to select the entire column.

Automatic adjustment

2. Choose Column and then AutoFit Selection from the Format menu. Here are the results:

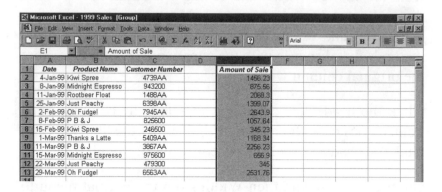

Excel has adjusted the width of the column to its longest entry.

3. Click the Save button to save your changes.

Changing row heights

You can adjust the height of rows the same way you adjust the width of columns. Simply drag the row header's bottom border up or down. You can also choose Row and then Height from the Format menu to make a selected row shorter or taller, or you can choose Row and AutoFit to adjust the height to the tallest entry in a selected row.

Wrapping Text in Cells

By default, Excel does not "wrap" text in a cell. As you saw, when you type a long text entry in a cell, that text spills over into the adjacent cells instead of wrapping (breaking) to another line within the same cell. But when you need to fit more than one line of text in the same cell for aesthetics, you can. For example, the Customer Number heading in the Quarterly worksheet is much longer than the other entries in column C. You could wrap the heading to two lines and then adjust the width of the column for a more pleasing look. Try this:

1. Click the row 1 header—the box containing the number 1—to select row 1.

2. Choose Cells from the Format menu. When the Format Cells dialog box appears, click the Alignment tab to display the options shown on the facing page.

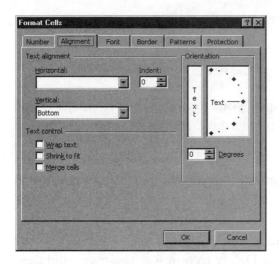

3. Click the Wrap Text check box to select that option, make sure Bottom is selected in the Vertical box, and then click OK. (Turning on the Bottom option ensures that any text in the row that doesn't wrap will sit at the bottom of its cell.)

4. Now point to the dividing line between the headers of columns C and D and drag to the left until the column is slightly wider than the word *Customer*. When you release the mouse button, the worksheet looks like this:

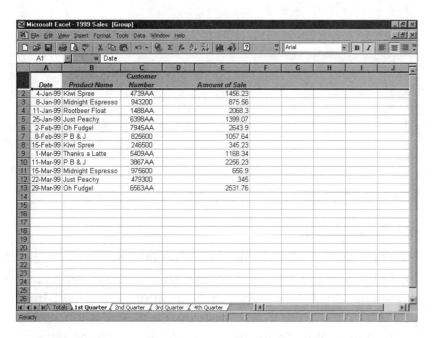

Rotating headings

To rotate the display of headings in a cell, first select the cell(s). Next choose Cells from the Format menu and click the Alignment tab. In the Orientation section, change the setting in the Degrees box or drag the indicator in the preview box to the desired angle. Then click OK. You can also display text vertically (from top to bottom) by clicking the box to the left of the preview box (the one that displays *Text* in a vertical format). To return headings to no rotation, click the preview box and then enter *0* in the Degrees box.

If Number has disappeared, don't panic. Simply choose Row and then AutoFit from the Format menu to ensure that the height of row 1 automatically adjusts to fit the lines of wrapping text.

While you're at it, wrap the headings in B1 and E1, too:

1. Use any of the techniques you learned in the previous section to decrease the width of column E so that its heading wraps to two lines.

Forcing text to wrap

2. You can't use this method to wrap the heading in column B because the width of that column is determined by the entries in B2:B13. Instead, force the heading to wrap by double-clicking cell B1, clicking an insertion point to the right of the word *Product*, pressing Delete to remove the space, and then pressing Alt+Enter to wrap the heading.

3. Press Enter. The results are shown below:

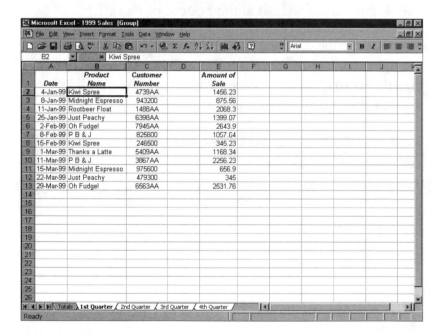

Adding Titles

You've learned how to format headings in simple ways by using buttons on the toolbar to change character formatting and alignment. In this section, we'll get more elaborate. First you'll give the quarterly worksheets a title and subtitle that really stand out by following the steps on the facing page.

1. Select rows 1, 2, and 3 by dragging down through their headers. Then choose Rows from the Insert menu. Excel inserts the number of rows you have selected—in this case, three—above the selection.

Inserting multiple rows

2. Press Home to remove the highlighting and move to cell A1, type *Preliminary Sales Analysis,* and press the Enter key.

3. In cell A2, type *1st Quarter, 1999* and press Enter.

4. Right-click cell A1 and choose Format Cells from the shortcut menu.

5. In the Format Cells dialog box, click the Font tab to display the options shown below:

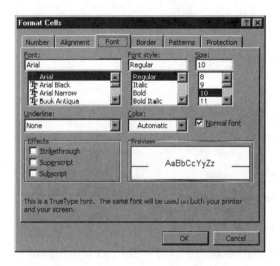

Don't worry if your fonts are different from ours. The list varies depending on the printer and applications you have installed.

6. Click Bold in the Font Style section, select 22 from the Size list, and click OK. Notice that the height of row 1 increases to accommodate the larger font.

7. Right-click cell A2 and again choose Format Cells from the shortcut menu.

8. In the Format Cells dialog box, click Bold Italic in the Font Style section, select 14 from the Size list, and click OK.

The Merge and Center
button

9. Now let's center the titles across columns A through E. Select A1:E1, click the Formatting toolbar's More Buttons button, and then click the Merge And Center button. Excel centers the title over the selected area and merges the four cells, but the title is still stored in cell A1.

10. Repeat step 9 for the subtitle, using the range A2:E2.

After you have finished all the formatting you want to apply to the quarterly sheets, you will need to ungroup the worksheets and then adjust the subheading of each sheet to reflect the correct quarter. We'll do this on page 53.

Specifying How Values Should Be Displayed

With the exception of the date values in column A, Excel has displayed the values you've entered so far in its default General format. With this format, Excel simply displays what you typed (or what it thinks you typed). For example, when you entered the dates in column A, Excel displayed them in a date format.

Excel provides several formats that you can use to change the way the values look. Try this:

The Comma Style button

1. Select E5 and click the Comma Style button on the Formatting toolbar's More Buttons palette. Excel formats the selected cell with a comma and two decimal places.

The Decrease Decimal and
Increase Decimal buttons

2. Click the Decrease Decimal button on the Formatting toolbar's More Buttons palette and then click it again to round the value in E5 to a whole dollar amount. Then click the Increase Decimal button twice to restore the two decimal places.

The Currency Style button

3. Finally, click the Currency Style button. Excel adds a dollar sign in front of the value. (If necessary, increase column E's width to view the results.)

4. To see the currency format for negative values, enter *1234* in cell F5, enter *-1234* in cell F6, select both values, click the Currency Style button, and click cell F7 to see the results shown on the facing page.

As well as adding a dollar sign, a comma, and two zeros to the right of the decimal point, Excel displays the negative value in parentheses and aligns it with the positive value above it.

When you click the Currency Style button, Excel applies its accounting format, in which the dollar sign is left-aligned, to the selected cells. However, other currency formats are available in the Format Cells dialog box, which also provides several other format options not available as buttons on the Formatting toolbar. You can apply these other formats by following these steps:

1. Select E6, right-click the selection, and choose Format Cells from the shortcut menu.

2. In the Format Cells dialog box, click the Number tab to display the options shown earlier on page 18.

3. Click each category to view its corresponding options. For example, click Number and note that you can change the number of decimal places, include a comma (1000 separator), and specify the way negative numbers are displayed.

4. Select Currency in the Category list and select the third option in the Negative Numbers list. Be sure the Decimal Places setting is 2 and that $ is selected in the Symbol edit box, and then click OK. Excel formats the selected entry with a dollar sign, a comma, and two decimal places, but as you can see on the next page, the dollar sign is adjacent to the value instead of left-aligned as it is in cell E5.

Underlying vs. displayed

After you apply a format, the value displayed in the cell might look different from the value in the formula bar. For example, 345.6789 is displayed in its cell as $345.68 after you apply the currency format. When performing calculations, Excel uses the value in the formula bar, not the displayed value.

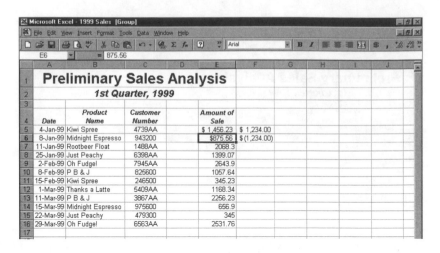

Formatting with styles

Excel applies a combination of formatting called the Normal style to your entries. It replaces Normal with a Currency, Comma, or Percent style when you click those buttons on the Formatting toolbar. You can modify Excel's styles by choosing Style from the Format menu, selecting the style from the Style Name list, and clicking the Modify button to display the Format Cells dialog box, where you can make your changes. If you want to create a custom style, enter a new name in the Style Name edit box, select or deselect the options in the Style Includes list, and use the Modify button to adjust any of the options. Click OK in the Style dialog box to apply the new style to the current selection, or click Add to add the style to the Style Name list without applying it, and then click OK. To apply the style later, select a cell or a range, choose Style from the Format menu, select the style from the Style Name drop-down list, and then click OK. To delete a style, select it from the Style Name drop-down list and click the Delete button.

While you're working with the Number tab of the Format Cells dialog box, you might want to explore Excel's date formats. In Chapter 1, you entered the dates in column A in a variety of formats and later we showed you how to make them all look the same. Let's see what other formats are available:

1. Select A5:A16, right-click the selection, and choose Format Cells from the shortcut menu. Excel displays the Number tab options with the cells' current format highlighted.

2. Select the 14-Mar format and click OK.

3. Return to the Format Cells dialog box and experiment with the other date types.

4. When you're ready, assign the 3/14/98 date type to A5:A16 and click OK.

Copying Formatting

In Excel, you can save a lot of formatting time by copying combinations of styles and formats from one cell to other cells. For example, if you format headings to be bold and centered, you can apply those styles to any cells in the worksheet simply by copying them. Let's give it a try:

1. Select cell F4, type *Type*, and press Enter.

2. Select cell A4, which contains a bold, italic, centered heading, and click the Format Painter button on the Standard toolbar's More Buttons palette.

The Format Painter button

3. Move the pointer to cell F4 and click once. Excel immediately applies the bold, italic, and centered styles to the selected cell.

Now let's format the remaining values in the Amount of Sale column as currency, this time copying the format from cell E5:

1. Select cell E5 and click the Format Painter button.

2. Next select E6:E16. When you release the mouse button, Excel applies the format from cell E5 to the selected range, adding dollar signs, commas, and two decimal places to the values. Your worksheet looks like this:

	A	B	C	D	E	F
1	**Preliminary Sales Analysis**					
2		*1st Quarter, 1999*				
3						
4	*Date*	*Product Name*	*Customer Number*		*Amount of Sale*	*Type*
5	1/4/99	Kiwi Spree	4739AA		$ 1,456.23	$ 1,234.00
6	1/8/99	Midnight Espresso	943200		$ 875.56	$ (1,234.00)
7	1/11/99	Rootbeer Float	1488AA		$ 2,068.30	
8	1/25/99	Just Peachy	6398AA		$ 1,399.07	
9	2/2/99	Oh Fudge!	7945AA		$ 2,643.90	
10	2/8/99	P B & J	025600		$ 1,057.64	
11	2/15/99	Kiwi Spree	246500		$ 345.23	
12	3/1/99	Thanks a Latte	5409AA		$ 1,168.34	
13	3/11/99	P B & J	3867AA		$ 2,256.23	
14	3/15/99	Midnight Espresso	975600		$ 656.90	
15	3/22/99	Just Peachy	479300		$ 345.00	
16	3/29/99	Oh Fudge!	6563AA		$ 2,531.76	
17						

To paint formatting into multiple ranges, first select a cell that contains the formatting you want to copy. Then double-click the Format Painter button and begin copying the formatting to all the ranges where you want the formatting to appear. When you've finished, click the Format Painter button again to toggle it off.

After all that work, you still have a little tidying up to do:

1. Delete the extraneous information in cells F4:F6.

2. Ungroup the active worksheets by holding down the Shift key and clicking the 1st Quarter tab.

Ungrouping worksheets

3. Activate the 2nd Quarter sheet and in the subheading, change *1st* to *2nd*. Then repeat this step to adjust the subheadings on the 3rd Quarter and 4th Quarter sheets.

From this simple example, you can see how easy it is to build complex combinations of formatting that can be applied with a couple of clicks of the mouse button.

Creating Templates

When you have spent some time creating a workbook, you can always "clone" it to create a new one. You open it, save it with a different name, and then plug in new values. However, Excel provides an even easier way to reuse workbooks. You can save any workbook as a *template*—a pattern that includes the structure, formatting, and other constant elements to be included in a particular type of workbook. Excel comes with several templates you can use as is or modify to meet your needs (see the adjacent tip). You can also create your own. As a demonstration, let's turn the workbook currently on your screen into a template:

1. Click the Save button to save the changes to 1999 Sales.

2. Choose Save As from the File menu to display the Save As dialog box shown earlier on page 23.

3. Enter *Sales* in the File Name edit box, and then click the arrow to the right of the Save As Type box and select Template from the drop-down list. The setting in the Save In box changes to Templates because by default, Excel saves the templates in the C:\Windows\Application Data\Microsoft\Templates folder. Leave this setting as it is.

4. Click Save. Excel closes the 1999 Sales workbook, and the name in the title bar changes to Sales to indicate that you are now working on the Sales template.

5. Activate the 1st Quarter sheet, select the subheading in cell A2, and replace *1999* with the word *Year*. Then select A5:E16 and press Delete to clear the contents of the cells without deleting their formats.

Excel's templates

Excel provides several templates that you can use to create documents such as invoices and purchase orders. To open a template, choose New from the File menu, click the Spreadsheet Solutions tab of the New dialog box, and click a template icon. If the Preview box indicates that the template is not yet installed, insert the installation CD-ROM and then click OK. Otherwise, double-click the template icon to open a workbook that uses the template as a pattern. (You may have to decide whether to enable the template's macros.) Often you can use the buttons on the template's toolbar to help you fill in the worksheet, and you can click the Display Example/Remove Example button to see an example of a completed worksheet. In addition, you can point to any cell with a red dot in its top right corner to see comments and instructions for that cell. You can customize a template—add a company logo or address, for example—by clicking the Customize button in the top right corner of the template. When the Customize sheet opens, enter the information you want to include in your custom template. To save a custom template, simply click the Lock/Save Sheet button, select the Lock And Save Template option, and enter a name for your template in the Save Template dialog box.

6. Repeat step 5 for the other quarterly sheets.

7. Activate the 1st Quarter worksheet, click the Save button to save the template, and then click the Close button at the right end of the menu bar to close the template without closing the program.

Now test your work by opening a new workbook based on the template:

1. Choose New from the File menu to display the New dialog box shown here:

Creating a workbook based on a template

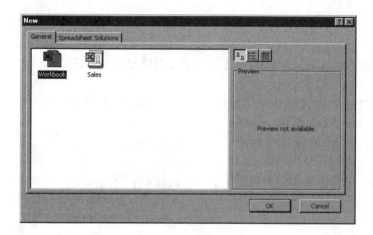

2. Double-click the Sales icon on the General tab to open a workbook called Sales1.

3. Save this workbook with the name *2000 Sales*, and then close it.

Voilà! You can now use this workbook to record sales for the year 2000.

Performing Calculations

3

In this chapter, you create a calculation area and explore some of Excel's functions, including the decision-making IF function. You use formulas to link worksheets, and finally, you print your worksheet and publish it as a Web page.

If you don't work in sales, you can adapt the techniques covered in this chapter to analyze other sources of income, such as service fees, subscriptions, or donations.

Worksheets created and concepts covered:

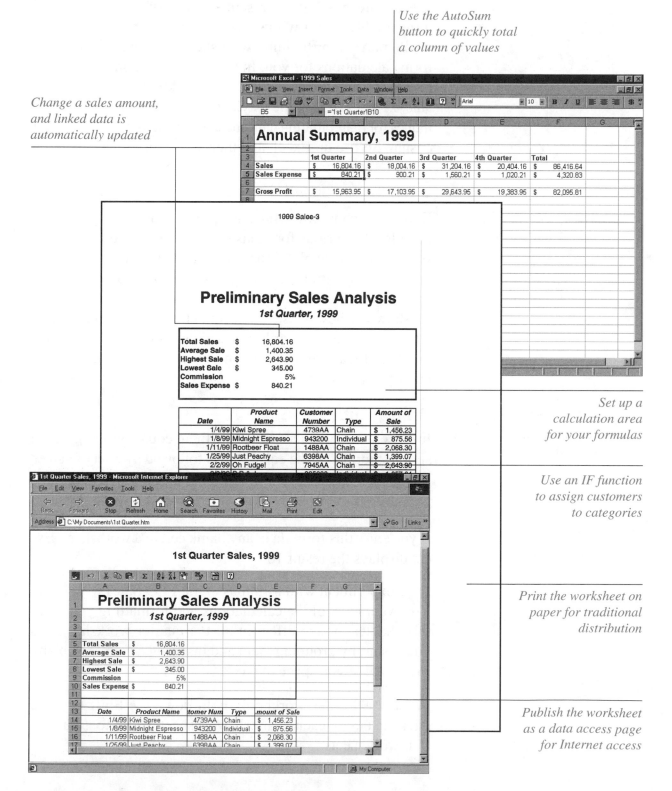

Use the AutoSum button to quickly total a column of values

Change a sales amount, and linked data is automatically updated

Set up a calculation area for your formulas

Use an IF function to assign customers to categories

Print the worksheet on paper for traditional distribution

Publish the worksheet as a data access page for Internet access

Chapters 1 and 2 covered some Excel basics, and you now know enough to create simple tables. But you are missing the essential piece of information that turns a table into a worksheet: how to enter formulas. The whole purpose of building worksheets is to have Excel perform calculations for you. In this chapter, we show you how to enter formulas in the 1999 Sales workbook so that you can analyze sales. Along the way, we cover some powerful techniques for manipulating data and a few principles of worksheet design. So fire up Excel, and then we'll get started.

Simple Calculations

Excel has many powerful functions that are a sort of short-hand for the various formulas used in mathematical, logical, statistical, financial, trigonometric, logarithmic, and other types of calculations. However, the majority of worksheets created with Excel involve simple arithmetic. In this section, we show you how to use four arithmetic operators (+, -, *, and /) to add, subtract, multiply, and divide, and then we introduce two Excel features with which you can quickly add sets of numeric values.

Doing Arithmetic

The equal (=) sign

In Excel, you begin a formula with an equal sign (=). In the simplest formulas, the equal sign is followed by a set of values separated by +, -, *, or /, such as

=5+3+2

If you enter this formula in any blank cell in a worksheet, Excel displays the result 10.

Let's experiment with formulas in the 1999 Sales workbook. You want most of the calculations and formatting you do in this chapter to take effect in all the quarter worksheets, so you'll start by grouping them and inserting a couple of blank rows to give you space to work:

1. In the 1999 Sales workbook, hold down the Shift key and click the tab for each quarter's worksheet in turn to group the four worksheets.

2. Drag through the headers for rows 4 and 5 of the 1st Quarter worksheet to select the two rows. Then right-click anywhere in the selected rows and choose Insert from the shortcut menu. Because you selected two rows, Excel inserts two blank rows on each of the four grouped worksheets, moving the tables down so that they begin in row 6.

Now you're ready to construct a formula in cell B5, using some of the values in the Amount of Sale column. You tell Excel to use a value simply by clicking the cell that contains it. Follow these steps:

1. Click cell B5 and type an equal sign followed by an opening parenthesis.

2. Click cell E7. Excel inserts the cell reference E7 in the cell and the formula bar.

   Entering cell references in formulas

3. Type a plus sign and click cell E8. Excel adds the cell reference E8 to the formula.

4. Continue to build the formula by typing plus signs and clicking cells E9, E10, and E11.

5. Type a closing parenthesis followed by a / (the division operator), and then type 5. The formula now looks like this:

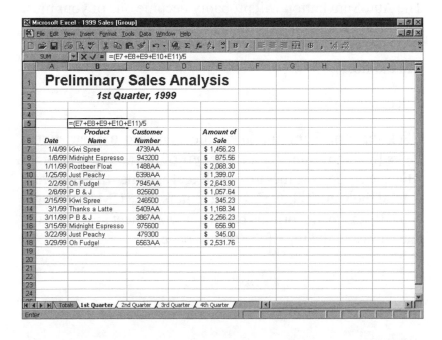

This formula tells Excel to first add the amounts in cells E7, E8, E9, E10, and E11 and then divide the result by 5 to obtain the average of the five amounts.

6. Click the Enter button. Excel displays the result of the formula, 1688.612, in cell B5.

You can use this same technique to create any simple formula. Start by typing an equal sign, then either enter a value or click the cell that contains the value, type the appropriate arithmetic operator, enter the next value, and so on. Unless you tell Excel to do otherwise, the program performs multiplication and division before addition and subtraction. If you need certain parts of the formula to be carried out in a different order, use parentheses as you did in this example to override the default order.

Order of precedence

Totaling Columns of Values

Although this method of creating a formula is simple enough, it would become tedious if you had to type and click in order to add a long series of values. Fortunately, Excel automates the addition process with a very useful button: the AutoSum button.

Using the AutoSum Button

The AutoSum button will probably become one of your most often-used Excel buttons. In fact, using this button is so easy that we'll dispense with explanations and simply show you what to do:

The AutoSum button

1. Select cell E19.

2. Click the AutoSum button on the Standard toolbar. Excel looks first above and then to the left of the active cell for an adjacent range of values to total. Excel assumes that you want to total the values above E19 and enters the SUM function in cell E19 and in the formula bar. Your worksheet looks like the one shown at the top of the facing page.

Displaying formulas

By default, Excel displays the results of formulas in cells, not their underlying formulas. To see the actual underlying formulas in the worksheet, choose Options from the Tools menu, display the View tab, select Formulas in the Window Options section, and click OK. Excel widens the cells so that you can see the formulas. To redisplay the results, simply deselect the Formulas option.

		Microsoft Excel - 1999 Sales [Group]									

=SUM(E7:E18)

	A	B	C	D	E	F	G	H	I	J
1	**Preliminary Sales Analysis**									
2	*1st Quarter, 1999*									
3										
4										
5		1688.612								
6	Date	Product Name	Customer Number		Amount of Sale					
7	1/4/99	Kiwi Spree	4739AA		$ 1,456.23					
8	1/8/99	Midnight Espresso	943200		$ 875.56					
9	1/11/99	Rootbeer Float	1488AA		$ 2,068.30					
10	1/25/99	Just Peachy	6398AA		$ 1,399.07					
11	2/2/99	Oh Fudge!	7945AA		$ 2,643.90					
12	2/8/99	P B & J	825600		$ 1,057.64					
13	2/15/99	Kiwi Spree	246500		$ 345.23					
14	3/1/99	Thanks a Latte	5409AA		$ 1,168.34					
15	3/11/99	P B & J	3867AA		$ 2,256.23					
16	3/15/99	Midnight Espresso	975600		$ 656.90					
17	3/22/99	Just Peachy	479300		$ 345.00					
18	3/29/99	Oh Fudge!	6563AA		$ 2,531.76					
19					=SUM(E7:E18)					
20										

3. Click the Enter button to enter the formula in cell E19. Excel displays the result $16,804.16—the sum of the values in E7:E18. (If necessary, widen the cell to see the value.)

That was easy. The AutoSum button serves you well whenever you want a total to appear at the bottom of a column or to the right of a row of values. But what if you want the total to appear elsewhere on the worksheet? Knowing how to create SUM functions from scratch gives you more flexibility.

Using the SUM Function

Let's go back and dissect the SUM function that Excel inserted in cell E19 when you clicked the AutoSum button so that you can examine the function's components.

With cell E19 selected, you can see the following entry in the formula bar:

=SUM(E7:E18)

Like all formulas, the SUM function begins with an equal sign (=). Next comes the function name in capital letters, followed by a set of parentheses enclosing the reference to the range containing the amounts you want to total. This reference is the SUM function's *argument*. An argument answers questions such as "What?" or "How?" and gives Excel the additional information it needs to perform the function. In the case of SUM, Excel needs only one piece of information—the references of the cells you want to total. As you'll see later, Excel

Arguments

might need several pieces of information to carry out other functions, and you enter an argument for each piece.

Creating a SUM function from scratch is not particularly difficult. For practice, follow these steps:

1. Select cell B5, and type this:

   =SUM(

   When you begin typing, the cell's old value is overwritten.

2. Select E7:E18 on the worksheet in the usual way. Excel inserts the reference E7:E18 after the opening parenthesis.

3. Type a closing parenthesis and then press Enter. Excel displays in cell B5 the total of the values in the Amount of Sale column—$16,804.16.

Referencing Formula Cells in Other Formulas

After you create a formula in one cell, you can use its result in other formulas simply by referencing its cell. To see how this works, follow these steps:

1. Select cell C5 and type an equal sign.

2. Click cell B5, which contains the SUM function you just entered, type a / (the division operator), and then type *12*.

3. Click the Enter button. Excel displays the result—the average of the invoice amounts—in cell C5. (We discuss an easier way to calculate averages on page 68.)

4. Press the Delete key to erase both the experimental formula and its result from cell C5.

Naming Cells and Ranges

Many of the calculations that you might want to perform on this worksheet—for example, calculating each sales amount as a percentage of total sales—will use the total you have calculated in cell B5. You could include a copy of the SUM function now in cell B5 in these other calculations, or you

Function names

When you type a function name, such as SUM, in the formula bar, you don't have to type it in capital letters. Excel capitalizes the function name for you when you complete the entry. If Excel does not respond in this way, you have probably entered the function name incorrectly.

could simply reference cell B5. The latter method seems quick and simple, but what if you subsequently move the formula in B5 to another location? Excel gives you a way to reference this formula no matter where on the worksheet you move it. You can assign cell B5 a name and then use the name in any calculations that involve the total.

Here's how to assign a name to a cell:

1. Select cell B5 and click the name box located to the left of the formula bar.

Assigning cell names

2. Type *Total* and press Enter. The name box now contains the cell's name instead of its reference. You can use either designation in formulas.

To see how Excel uses the names you assign, try this:

1. Select cell E19, which currently contains the SUM function you inserted earlier in the chapter.

2. Type *=Total* and press Enter. The worksheet does not appear to change, but now instead of two SUM functions, the worksheet contains only one. You have told Excel to assign the value of the cell named Total, which contains the SUM function, to cell E19.

You can also assign names to ranges. Let's use a different method to assign the name Amount to the cells containing amounts in column E:

Assigning range names

1. Select E7:E18 and choose Name and then Define from the Insert menu to display this dialog box:

Excel's name suggestions

When you choose Name and then Define from the Insert menu to name a cell or a range of cells, Excel looks above and to the left of the selected cell or range to find a name. Keep this information in mind when you enter labels in your worksheet. If you plan on defining names for certain cells, enter a label above or to the left of the cell(s) that Excel can readily use as a name.

The reference '1st Quarter'!$E$7:$E$18 displayed in the Refers To edit box is an absolute reference to the range E7:E18 on the 1st Quarter sheet of the current workbook. (For an explanation of absolute references, see page 75.)

2. Replace Excel's suggested name with *Amount* and press Enter.

Now let's replace the range reference in the SUM function in cell B5 with the new range name. (You can't do this while the worksheets are grouped.) Follow these steps:

1. First hold down the Shift key and click the 1st Quarter tab to ungroup the sheets. Then click B5 to select it and to display its contents in the formula bar.

2. Drag through the E7:E18 reference in the formula bar to highlight it. (While you're dragging, Excel displays the reference in blue and outlines the actual range with a blue border. See the tip on page 73 to find out why.)

Inserting named cells in a formula

3. Choose Name and then Paste from the Insert menu to display this dialog box:

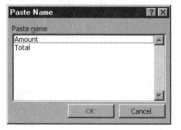

Name conventions

Certain rules apply when you name cells or ranges. Although you can use a number within the name, you must start the name with a letter, an underscore, or a backslash. Spaces are not allowed within the name, so you should use underscore characters to represent spaces. For example, you cannot use 1999 as a name, but you can use Totals_1999.

4. Select Amount and click OK. Excel replaces the range reference with the name assigned to the range, and the formula bar now reads =*SUM(Amount)*.

5. Click the Enter button. The total in cell B5 remains the same as before, even though you've changed the formula.

6. Click the Save button to save your work.

From now on, we won't give you specific instructions to save your work, but you should get in the habit of saving often, perhaps after working through each example.

Creating a Calculation Area

Before we discuss other calculations you might want to perform with this worksheet, let's look at ways to format your information to make the results of calculations stand out from the data. As your worksheets grow in complexity, you'll find that paying attention to such details will keep you oriented and help others understand your results.

Usually when you create a worksheet, you are interested not so much in the individual pieces of information as in the results of the calculations you perform on the pieces. The current worksheet is not much bigger than one screen, but often worksheets of this type include many screenfuls of information. It's a good idea to design your worksheets so that the important information is easily accessible and in a predictable location. For these reasons, we suggest that you leave room in the top left corner of your worksheets for a calculation area. This habit is useful for the following reasons:

- You don't have to scroll around looking for totals and other results.   ← **Advantages**

- You can print just the first page of a worksheet to get a report of the most pertinent information.

- You can easily jump to the calculation area from anywhere on the worksheet by pressing Ctrl+Home to move to cell A1.

To see firsthand how helpful this can be, create an area at the top of each of the grouped quarter sheets of the 1999 Sales workbook for a set of calculations. Start by freeing up some more space below the worksheet title:

1. Group the four quarter sheets and then select A6:E19.

2. Then use the Cut and Paste buttons to move the selection to A13:E26. (Leave the entry in B5 where it is.)

3. Press Ctrl+Home. Your screen now looks like the one shown on the next page.

Jumping to named cells

To move quickly to a named cell, press the F5 key. When Excel displays the Go To dialog box, select the name of the cell you want to move to and click OK.

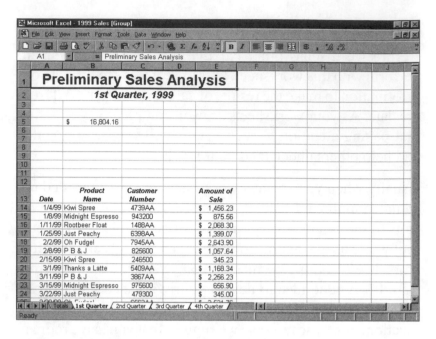

Now you need to make the calculation area stand out. With Excel, you can get really fancy, using colored fonts and shading to draw attention to calculation results. For now, though, let's place a simple border around the calculation area:

1. Select A4:E11 and choose Cells from the Format menu.

2. When the Format Cells dialog box appears, click the Border tab to display these options:

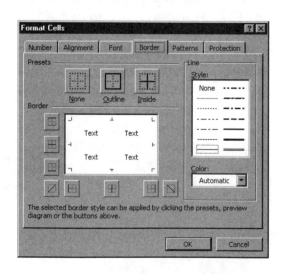

3. In the Style list of the Line section, select the fifth option in the column on the right. In the Presets section, select Outline.

Page breaks

If you want to print the calculation area on one page and the supporting data on another, or if you need to control where the pages break in a multipage worksheet, select the cell below the row and to the right of the column at which you want Excel to break the page, and choose Page Break from the Insert menu. Excel indicates the break by using a dashed line. To remove a manual page break, select the cell immediately below and to the right of the page break, and choose Remove Page Break from the Insert menu. To remove all the page breaks in a worksheet, select the entire document by clicking the square in the top left corner of the worksheet (at the intersection of the row and column headers), and choose Remove Page Break.

4. Now click the Patterns tab to display these options:

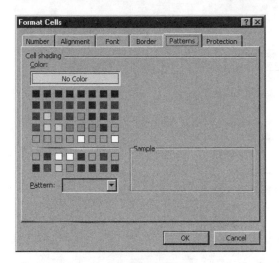

5. If you have a color printer, simply pick a light color for the background of the selected cells and then click OK. (We left the background white so that our screen graphics would be legible.)

Now let's add another touch:

1. Select A5:A10.

2. Click the Bold button on the Formatting toolbar.

Why did we tell you to select the empty cells before applying the Bold style? Try this:

1. Select cell A5, type *Total Sales*, and click the Enter button. The new heading is bold because you already applied the Bold style to cell A5.

2. Without moving the selection, choose Column and AutoFit Selection from the Format menu to adjust the width of column A to the longest entry. (From now on, use this technique to adjust columns as necessary to see their contents.)

3. For good measure, select cell B5, click the Format Painter button, and select B6:B10 to copy the currency format to that range of cells.

4. Press Ctrl+Home. The next page shows the results.

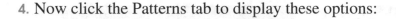

Preformatting cells

Buttons for borders and shading

To add a border around a selected cell or range, click the arrow to the right of the Borders button on the Formatting toolbar to display a palette of options (including borders on the left, right, top, or all sides). Then click the button that adds the border you want. To fill a selected cell or range with a color, click the arrow to the right of the Fill Color button on the Formatting toolbar. When Excel displays a palette of colors, click the one you want. (The palettes include a No Borders button and a No Fill button, which you can use to remove borders and shading from selections.)

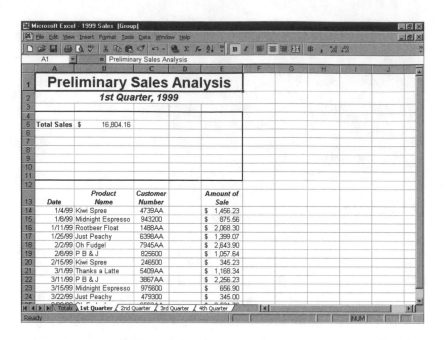

More Calculations

Let's perform some more calculations on the sales data, starting with the average sale.

Averaging Values

To find the average of the invoices in this worksheet, you can build a formula that includes Excel's AVERAGE function. To avoid making errors while typing function names and to make sure you include all the arguments needed for the calculation, you'll want to use the Paste Function button. Follow these steps:

1. Select cell A6, type *Average Sale*, and click the Enter button. (If the heading wraps to two lines, right-click the row 6 header, choose Format Cells from the shortcut menu, click the Alignment tab, turn off Wrap Text, and click OK.) Then widen column A.

The Paste Function button

2. Select cell B6 and click the Paste Function button on the Standard toolbar. Excel displays the Paste Function dialog box shown on the facing page, and the Office Assistant may offer assistance.

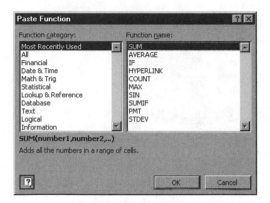

Below the list boxes, the dialog box displays the syntax of the function selected in the Function Name list. The syntax tells you how the function must be entered after the = sign in the formula bar. You will replace the placeholders between parentheses in the syntax (in this case, number1,number2,...) with the actual values you want Excel to use.

3. If necessary, click No in the Office Assistant's box. Then select AVERAGE in the Function Name list and click OK. Excel displays this formula palette:

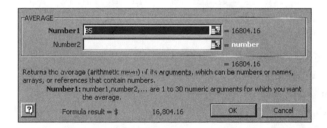

The palette displays a definition of the function and its arguments. In the Number1 edit box, you can enter a number, cell reference, name, formula, or another function.

4. Select E14:E25 in the worksheet to add its name, Amount, as the formula's argument. As you begin your selection, the palette collapses, and when you release the mouse button, the palette expands again. Excel displays =AVERAGE(Amount) in the formula bar and the result of the formula at the bottom of the palette, which is shown on the next page.

Conditional formatting

To monitor a worksheet, you can use conditional formatting to highlight a cell that meets certain criteria. For example, you can display a cell's value in magenta if it is over 200,000. To apply this type of formatting, select the cell and choose Conditional Formatting from the Format menu. Select a condition from the second drop-down list and enter conditional parameters in the appropriate edit boxes. Then click Format, select the formatting to be used to highlight the cell, and click OK twice. When the value in the selected cell meets the condition you've set, Excel highlights the cell with the specified formatting. If you want to delete conditional formatting, select the cell, choose Conditional Formatting from the Format menu, click Delete, select the condition, and click OK twice.

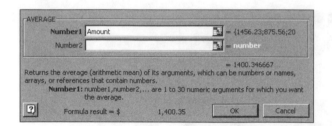

5. Click OK to enter the formula in cell B6. Press Ctrl+Home to see the results, $1,400.35, displayed in cell B6.

Identifying Highest and Lowest Values

Excel provides two functions that instantly identify the highest and lowest values in a group. To understand the benefits of these functions, imagine that the 1st Quarter worksheet contains data from not 12 but 112 customers! Let's start with the highest sale:

1. Select cell A7, type *Highest Sale*, press the Right Arrow key to confirm the entry and to select cell B7.

2. Click the Edit Formula button (the = at the left end of the formula bar). Excel enters = in the formula bar and replaces the name box to the left of the formula bar with the function name box.

3. Click the arrow to the right of the function name box. Then select MAX (for *maximum*) from the drop-down list. (If the function you want is already displayed, you can simply click it.) Excel then displays the formula palette shown here:

```
┌─ MAX ──────────────────────────────────────────────────────────┐
│         Number1  36                              [≣] = 1400.346667 │
│         Number2                                   [≣] = number     │
│                                                    = 1400.346667    │
│  Returns the largest value in a set of values. Ignores logical values and text. │
│                                                                   │
│         Number1: number1,number2,... are 1 to 30 numbers, empty cells, logical values, or │
│                  text numbers for which you want the maximum.     │
│  [?]    Formula result = $         1,400.35        [  OK  ]  [ Cancel ] │
└──────────────────────────────────────────────────────────────────┘
```

4. Select E14:E25 on the worksheet. The formula bar displays =MAX(Amount), and Excel displays the result of the formula at the bottom of the palette.

Moving dialog boxes

To enter a cell or range reference in a dialog box, you can click the cell or select the range in the worksheet. If the dialog box obscures the desired cell or range, simply move the dialog box out of the way by pointing to its title bar, holding down the mouse button, and dragging until you can see the part of the worksheet you're interested in. Many dialog boxes also contain Collapse buttons (the buttons with the red arrow) that shrink the dialog box so that you can view more of the worksheet.

5. Click OK to close the formula palette. Excel enters the highest sale amount, $2,643.90, in cell B7.

To determine the lowest sale, you'll use Excel's AutoCalculate feature:

1. Select cell A8, type *Lowest Sale*, and press Enter.

Using AutoCalculate

2. Select E14:E25 and notice that Excel has entered the sum of the values in the range in the AutoCalculate area of the status bar at the bottom of the window.

3. Right-click the AutoCalculate area and select Min from the shortcut menu. Excel displays the result, $345.00, in the AutoCalculate area.

4. Now that you know the result, select cell B8, type *345*, and press Enter.

You can also use AutoCalculate to quickly apply other functions, such as AVERAGE and COUNT, to a selected range.

Calculating with Names

The salespeople at the Cream of the Crop ice cream company all earn commission. As a gross indicator of sales expenses, you can use the Total Sales value in cell B5 to calculate the total sales commission. Here's how:

1. In cell A9, type *Commission* and press Tab.

2. Type *6%* and click the Enter button.

3. With cell B9 still active, choose Name and then Define from the Insert menu. Excel scans the adjacent cells and suggests the name *Commission*. Click OK.

Now you'll use the commission percentage in a formula that will calculate the total commission:

1. Select cell A10, type *Sales Expense*, and press Tab.

2. With cell B10 selected, type the formula *=Total*Commission* and press Enter. Excel multiplies the value in the cell named

A function for every task

Excel provides many functions for common business and financial tasks—some of them quite complex. To get more information about a function, first display the Help window, and then type *worksheet_function* on the Index tab and click Search. In the Choose A Topic list, click a specific function (for example, RATE). Excel then displays a description of the function, its syntax, and any other information that is pertinent in the pane on the right.

Total (B5) by the value in the cell named Commission (B9) and displays the result, $1,008.25, in cell B10.

3. Now select cell B9, type *5%*, and press Enter. Instantly, the value in cell B10 changes to reflect the new commission rate, as shown here:

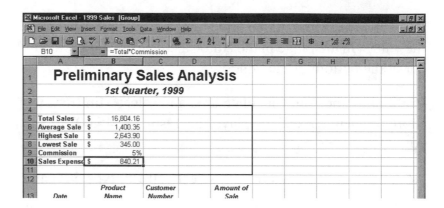

If a hundred calculations throughout the worksheet referenced the cell named Commission, Excel would adjust all their results to reflect this one change. Powerful stuff!

Formulas That Make Decisions

There will be times when you want Excel to carry out one task under certain circumstances and another task if those circumstances don't apply. To give this kind of instruction to Excel, you use the IF function.

In its simplest form, the IF function tests the value of a cell and does one thing if the test is positive (true) and another if the test is negative (false). It requires three arguments: the test, the action to perform if the test is true, and the action to perform if the test is false. You supply the arguments one after the other within the function's parentheses, separating them with commas (no spaces). Try this:

1. Select cell D5, type the following, and then press Enter:

=IF(B5=0,"TRUE","FALSE")

Excel checks whether the value in cell B5 is zero (the test). Because it isn't zero, Excel ignores TRUE (the action to

---

The IF function →

Logical operators

Here is a list of operators you can use with the IF function:

= < > <> >= <=

You can also use AND and OR to combine two or more tests. The function

=IF(AND(B4=0,B5>0),"Yes","No")

displays Yes only if both tests are true. The function

=IF(OR(B4=0,B5>0),"Yes","No")

displays Yes if either test is true.

perform if the test is true) and in cell D5 displays FALSE (the action to perform if the test is false).

2. Double-click cell D5. (Notice that Excel changes the B5 reference to blue and puts a matching blue border around cell B5—see the tip below for more information.) Drag through =0 to highlight it, type<*100000*, and press Enter. The entry in cell D5 instantly changes from FALSE to TRUE, because the value in cell B5 is less than one hundred thousand; that is, the test is true.

3. Now select cell D5 and press Delete to clear the cell.

In this example, the test Excel performed was a simple evaluation of the value in a cell. However, you can also build tests that involve other functions. Recall that the last two characters of the customer numbers in column C of the worksheet indicate whether the sale was made to a large chain store or to an individually owned store. Suppose you want to assign each customer number to a Chain or Individual category so that you can compare the sales for the two store types. Follow these steps:

1. Select cell D13, enter the heading *Type*, and press Enter.

2. In cell D14, type the following and click the Enter button:

=IF(RIGHT(C14,2)="AA","Chain","Individual")

You have told Excel to look at the two characters at the right end of the value in cell C14 and if they are AA, to enter *Chain* in cell D14. If they are not AA, Excel is to enter *Individual*. The result is shown here:

	A	B	C	D	E
2			*1st Quarter, 1999*		
3					
4					
5	Total Sales	$	16,804.16		
6	Average Sale	$	1,400.35		
7	Highest Sale	$	2,643.90		
8	Lowest Sale	$	345.00		
9	Commission		5%		
10	Sales Expense	$	840.21		
11					
12					
13	Date	Product Name	Customer Number	Type	Amount of Sale
14	1/4/99	Kiwi Spree	4739AA	Chain	$ 1,456.23
15	1/8/99	Midnight Espresso	943200		$ 875.56

The Range Finder

When you double-click a cell to edit a formula, Excel's Range Finder feature displays any of the formula's cells or ranges of cells in a particular color and places a matching color border around the actual cell or range. The Range Finder is a useful means of double-checking the references in your formulas.

Copying Formulas

The IF function you just entered is arduous to type, even for good typists. Fortunately, you don't have to enter it more than once. By using a simple mouse operation called *AutoFill*, you can copy the formula into the cells below, like this:

AutoFill

1. With D14 selected, position the pointer over the tiny square, called the *fill handle,* in the bottom right corner of the cell.

2. When the pointer changes to a black cross, hold down the left mouse button and drag down to cell D25. When you release the mouse button, Excel copies the formula from D14 into the highlighted cells. Here are the results:

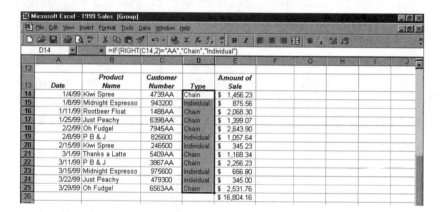

3. Select cell D15 and look at the formula in the formula bar. Excel has changed the original formula

   =IF(RIGHT(C14,2)="AA","Chain","Individual")

   to

   =IF(RIGHT(C15,2)="AA","Chain","Individual")

   When you used AutoFill, Excel changed the reference so that it refers to cell C15 as its argument, not C14. Why?

Relative references

By default, Excel uses *relative references* in its formulas. Relative references refer to cells by their position in relation to the cell containing the formula. So when you copied the formula in cell D14 to cell D15, Excel changed the reference from C14 to C15—the cell in the same row and one column to the left of the cell containing the formula. If you were to copy the formula in cell D14 to F14, Excel would change the reference from C14 to E14 so that the formula would continue to reference the cell in the same relative position.

When you don't want a reference to be copied as a relative reference, as it was in these examples, you need to use an *absolute reference*. Absolute references refer to cells by their fixed position in the worksheet. To make a reference absolute, you add dollar signs before its column letter and row number. For example, to change the reference C4:C9 to an absolute reference, you would enter it as $C$4:$C$9. You could then copy a formula that contained this reference anywhere on the worksheet and it would always refer to the range C4:C9.

◄—————————— Absolute references

References can also be partially relative and partially absolute. For example, $C4 has an absolute column reference and a relative row reference, and C$4 has a relative column reference and an absolute row reference.

Linking Worksheets with Formulas

Earlier you transferred the results of a SUM function to a different cell simply by referencing the cell containing the function (see page 62). You can just as easily transfer a function's results from one worksheet to another, thereby linking the two worksheets so that any changes in the source worksheet are immediately reflected in the linked worksheet. In this section, you'll set up the four quarter worksheets first so that they contain different sets of invoice data, and then you'll use the Totals worksheet to build some summary information. Let's get going:

1. Hold down the Shift key, click the 1st Quarter tab to ungroup the quarter worksheets, and then click the 2nd Quarter tab.

2. Select cell A14, type *4/6/99*, press Enter, type *4/13/99*, and press Enter again.

3. Select A14:A15 and drag the fill handle down to cell A25. Based on the interval between the dates in the two selected cells, Excel calculates what the entries in each cell you select should be, and when you release the mouse button, Excel fills the selected range with a set of dates one week apart.

Text values as arguments

When entering text values as arguments in a formula, you must enclose them in quotation marks. Otherwise, Excel thinks the text is a name and displays the error value #NAME? in the cell. For example,

=RIGHT("Excel",2)

gives the value "el," but

=RIGHT(Excel,2)

results in an error—unless the range name *Excel* happens to be assigned to a cell or range in the worksheet.

4. Next select cell E14, increment its entry by $100, and press Enter. Repeat this step for the entries in E15:E25.

5. Repeat steps 2, 3, and 4 for the 3rd Quarter worksheet, using starting dates of 7/5/99 and 7/12/99 and incrementing the sales amounts by $200. Then do the same for the 4th Quarter worksheet with 10/7/99 and 10/14/99 and $300.

Why haven't the values in the calculation area changed? The formulas in B5:B10 reference the Amount and Total names, which you applied to cells on the 1st Quarter sheet. Follow these steps to quickly create new names:

1. Choose Name and then Define from the Insert menu, select Amount, change the name to *Amount 1*, and click Add.

2. Change the Names In Workbook entry to *Amount 2*, change ='*1st* in the Refers To entry to ='*2nd*, and click Add.

3. Repeat step 2 to create an *Amount 3* name that refers to the 3rd Quarter sheet and an *Amount 4* name that refers to the 4th Quarter sheet.

4. Repeat steps 2 and 3 to create Total names for the four sheets.

5. Delete the original Amount and Total names and click OK.

6. Back in the workbook, replace the names in all the formulas on the quarter sheets with the correct names for the active worksheet. (For example, on the 1st Quarter sheet, replace Amount with Amount 1 and Total with Total 1.)

Now that the quarter sheets contain different sets of data, you can turn your attention to the Totals worksheet:

1. Activate the Totals worksheet, press Ctrl+Home, and enter *Annual Summary, 1999* in cell A1. Then make this title bold and left-aligned, and change its size to 22.

2. In cell B3, type *1st Quarter*, click the Enter button, and drag the fill handle to cell E3. The AutoFill feature increments the number in the selection and enters the headings 2nd Quarter, 3rd Quarter, and 4th Quarter.

The Fill command

You can use the Fill command to copy entries into a range of adjacent cells. Select the cell whose contents and formats you want to copy, drag through the adjacent range, and choose Fill from the Edit menu. How Excel copies the cell is determined by the shape of the selection and the command you choose from the Fill submenu. For example, selecting cells below an entry and choosing Down copies the entry down a range; selecting cells to the right of an entry and choosing Right copies the entry to the right; and so on. Three related commands are also available on this submenu: Across Worksheets copies entries to the equivalent cells in a group of selected worksheets (to select the worksheets, hold down Ctrl and click each sheet's tab); Series fills the selection with a series of values or dates; and Justify distributes the contents of the active cell evenly in the cells of the selected range.

3. Enter *Total* in cell F3, *Sales* in cell A4, *Sales Expense* in cell A5, and *Gross Profit* in cell A7.

4. Make the headings in row 3 and column A bold, and then select columns A through F and change their widths to 15.

5. Select B4:F7 and format the range as currency.

To link the Total Sales formulas on the four quarter sheets to the Totals sheet, follow these steps:

1. Select cell B4, type =, activate the 1st Quarter sheet, click cell B5, and press Tab.

2. Repeat step 1 to link cell C4 on the Totals sheet with cell B5 on the 2nd Quarter sheet, cell D4 on the Totals sheet with cell B5 on the 3rd Quarter sheet, and cell E4 on the Totals sheet with cell B5 on the 4th Quarter sheet.

3. In cell F4 on the Totals sheet, click the AutoSum button, and click the Enter button.

4. Now link the Sales Expense formulas in cell B10 on the four quarter sheets to cells B5:E5 on the Totals sheet, and use the AutoSum button to obtain the total sales expense for the year.

5. Enter the gross profit on the Totals sheet by selecting cell B7, entering *=B4-B5*, and using AutoFill to copy the formula to C7:F7. Here are the results:

Now test the links by following these steps:

1. Suppose the summer months were unusually hot, resulting in record sales for the third quarter. Activate the 3rd Quarter worksheet and increment all the sales amounts by $1,000.

More about AutoFill

You can copy information from one area of your worksheet to another using two methods: Auto-Fill, and copy and paste. These methods produce similar results unless the entry you are copying contains a number that can be incremented, such as in the 1st Quarter heading, or the cell contains an entry from a custom list. If the cell contains a number that can be incremented, using Auto-Fill copies the entry and increments the number—for example, 1st Quarter becomes 2nd Quarter, 3rd Quarter, and so on. If the cell contains an entry from a custom list, Excel fills the cells with other entries from that list. You define a custom list by choosing Options from the Tools menu, clicking the Custom Lists tab, selecting NEW LIST in the Custom Lists box, and typing the list's entries in the List Entries box. (You can also click an insertion point in the Import List From Cells edit box, select a range containing the entries, and click the Import button to import the entries as a list.) After you click OK, you can enter the list in consecutive cells of any worksheet by typing one of the entries and dragging the fill handle. This feature is invaluable if you frequently create worksheets involving lists of the same entries, such as part numbers or employee names.

2. Return to the Totals worksheet and compare the new totals with those in the preceding graphic. The linking formulas have done their jobs and faithfully updated the Totals worksheet to reflect the new information in the source worksheets.

Printing and Publishing Worksheets

If your primary purpose in learning Excel is to be able to manipulate your own information, your worksheets might never need to leave your computer. If, on the other hand, you want to share your worksheets with others, you will probably need to either print them or publish them on your organization's intranet. Now is a good time to discuss how to print or publish an Excel worksheet.

Previewing Worksheets

Usually, you'll want to preview a worksheet before you print or publish it to make sure that single-page sheets fit neatly on the page and that multi-page sheets break in logical places. Follow these steps to get a bird's-eye view of a worksheet:

The Print Preview button

1. Activate the 1st Quarter worksheet and click the Print Preview button on the Standard toolbar. The print preview window opens, with a miniature version of the printed worksheet displayed, as shown here:

Page break preview

When you click the Page Break Preview button on the Print Preview toolbar, Excel switches to page break view. You can then adjust where your worksheet's information breaks into pages. Cells that will be printed on the active page appear in white, while cells outside the active page appear in gray. To adjust a page break, simply drag the dotted line that represents the page break to its new location. To return to print preview, click the Print Preview button. To return to normal view, simply choose Normal from the View menu.

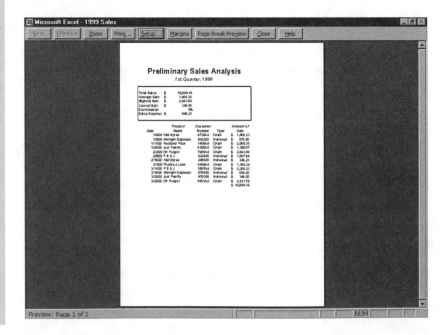

2. Move the mouse pointer over the page. The pointer changes to a small magnifying glass.

3. To examine part of the page in more detail, move the magnifying glass over that part and click the mouse button. Excel zooms in on that portion of the page, magnifying it so that it is readable.

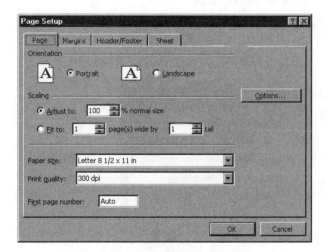

Zooming in on the page

4. Click again to zoom out.

Setting Up the Pages

You can change the worksheet's orientation, adjust margins, add a header or footer, and make other adjustments in the Page Setup dialog box. In print preview, you can open this dialog box by following these steps:

1. Click the Setup button on the Print Preview toolbar to display a Page Setup dialog box that looks something like this one:

Your dialog box might differ slightly, depending on the type of printer you have. Notice that on the Page tab, you can set the orientation of your printed worksheet and control the scale at which it is printed.

2. Now click the Margins tab to display the options shown on the next page.

Adjusting margins in print preview

In addition to using the Margins tab of the Page Setup dialog box, you can also adjust margins and column widths in print preview. Click the Margins button on the Print Preview toolbar to display guidelines that you can manually move to increase or decrease the margins and columns. Click the Margins button again to turn off the guidelines.

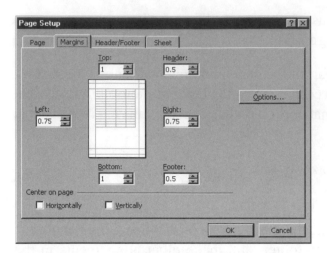

3. Change the Top setting to 2 inches. Then in the Center On Page section, click Horizontally to center the worksheet horizontally on the page. The preview box in the center of the dialog box shows you the effects of your changes.

Now let's add a header to the worksheet:

1. Click the Header/Footer tab to display these Header/Footer options:

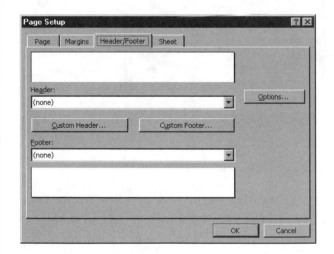

2. Click the arrow to the right of the Header box and select 1999 Sales from the drop-down list.

3. Click the arrow to the right of the Footer box and select Page 1.

By default, Excel will center the specified text at the top and bottom of the page. If you want a different arrangement, you

Custom headers and footers

To create a customized header or footer, you can click the Custom Header or Custom Footer button to display a dialog box in which you can type the text you want. The buttons in the Header and Footer dialog boxes add codes that do the following:

&[Page]	Adds current page number
&[Pages]	Inserts total number of pages
&[Date]	Adds current date
&[Time]	Adds current time
&[File]	Adds filename
&[Tab]	Adds sheet name

You can format the header and footer by selecting the text or code you want to format, clicking the font button (the capital A) to display the Font dialog box, and making your selections.

can use the Custom Header and Custom Footer buttons to create customized headers and footers; see the tip on the facing page.

Here's how to mark the cell boundaries with gridlines:

1. Click the Sheet tab to display these options:

← Displaying gridlines

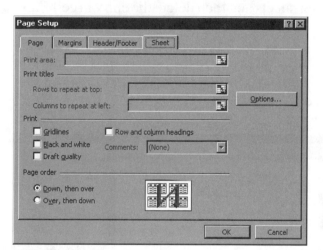

2. Select the Gridlines check box in the Print section and then click OK. Back in print preview, the worksheet now looks like the one shown here:

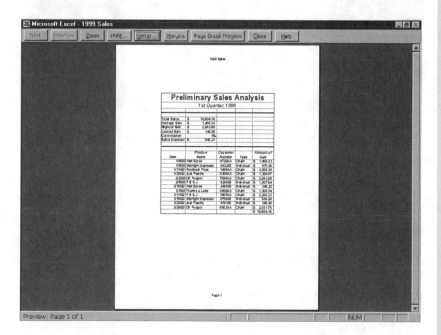

Controlling printing

On the Sheet tab of the Page Setup dialog box, you can enter a specific range as the print area of the worksheet. For example, you might want to print only the range containing the results of your calculations. You could select this range before printing and then tell Excel in the Print dialog box to print only the selection, but if you often print the same range, specifying it as the print area is more efficient. (You can also select a range of cells and choose Print Area and then Set Print Area from the File menu. Clear the print area by choosing Print Area and then Clear Print Area.) You can use the options in the Print Titles section of the Sheet tab to tell Excel to repeat column and row headings on multi-page worksheets. And you can use options in the Page Order section to tell Excel in what order to print multi-page worksheets.

Excel has added gridlines to the active area of the worksheet—all the cells that contain entries. This isn't exactly the effect you want.

3. Click Setup again, deselect the Gridlines option on the Sheet tab, and click OK. Then click Close to return to normal view.

4. Group the quarter sheets and then delete the entry in cell E26.

The Borders and All Borders buttons

5. Next select A13:E25, click the Formatting toolbar's More Buttons button, click the arrow to the right of the Borders button, and then click the All Borders button. Click the Print Preview button to see these results:

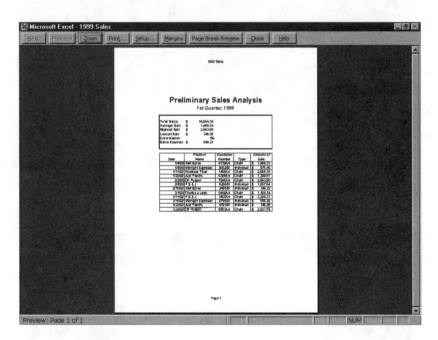

6. Click the Close button on the Print Preview toolbar to return to normal view.

7. Ungroup the four quarter worksheets.

Printing Worksheets

The Print button

When you are ready to print, you can click the Print button on the Standard toolbar. If you want to change the default print settings, you can choose Print from the File menu. Follow the steps at the top of the facing page to try the second method.

1. Choose Print from the File menu to display these options:

In this dialog box, you can specify exactly what you want to print, from a single cell to an entire workbook. You can also specify the number of copies you want to print, and, if you haven't already paid a visit to print preview, you can activate it directly by clicking the Preview button.

Specifying what to print

2. To send the worksheet to the printer, click OK. You can then evaluate the results of your efforts on paper.

Publishing on an Intranet or the World Wide Web

You can convert an Excel workbook into a set of Web pages that can be stored on your organization's intranet or Web server so that it can be viewed with a Web browser such as Internet Explorer. This type of publishing is made possible by a coding system called HTML (HyperText Markup Language). In this section, we show you how to preview the workbook you have created to see how it will look when converted to a Web page. Then we'll show you how to save the workbook as an HTML document. Follow these steps:

1. With the 1st Quarter worksheet of the 1999 Sales workbook open on your screen, choose Web Page Preview from the File menu. Internet Explorer starts, converts the workbook file temporarily to HTML, and displays it as shown on the following page.

Printer setup

When you installed Windows, the Setup program also installed the driver (the control program) for the printer attached to your computer. If you also have access to other printers, you can install their drivers by using the Add Printer Wizard in the Printers folder. (Choose Settings and then Printers from the Start menu.) The installed printers can all be accessed by Excel, but only one at a time. To switch printers, choose Print from the File menu, click the arrow to the right of the Name box in the Printer section of the Print dialog box, select the printer you want to use, and click OK.

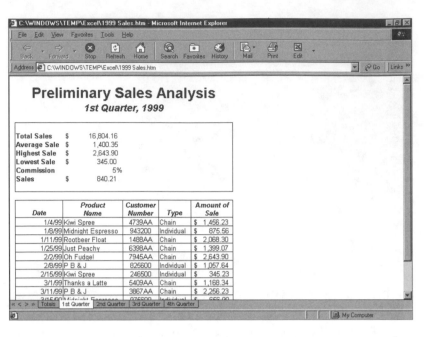

Viewing worksheets

2. Use the tabs at the bottom of the screen to see all the work-sheets, and then click the Close button to return to Excel.

   Let's convert the 1st Quarter worksheet to HTML:

Saving as HTML

1. Save the workbook and then choose Save As Web Page from the File menu to display this dialog box:

Publishing part of a worksheet

To publish part of a workbook as a Web page, first select the range you want to publish. Next choose Save As Web Page from the File menu and click the Selection option in the Save section of the dialog box. (Excel displays the range reference to the right of the Selection option.) Then continue the save operation as described in the adjacent exercise.

2. Click the Selection: Sheet option to save just the active sheet, replace the default name in the File Name edit box with *1st Quarter*, and click the Publish button to display the dialog box on the facing page.

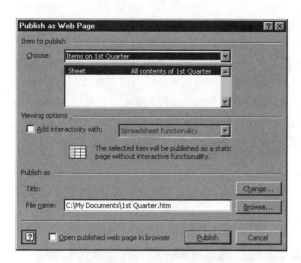

3. Click the Add Interactivity With check box to allow people who are viewing the worksheet to be able to change its values and formulas.

Adding interactivity

4. Click the Change button to the right of Title in the Publish As section, type *1st Quarter Sales, 1999* as the title of the worksheet's page, and click OK.

5. Finally, check that the path in the File Name edit box reflects the location where you want to store the HTML file, check that the Open Published Web Page In Browser check box is selected, and click Publish. Here's what you see:

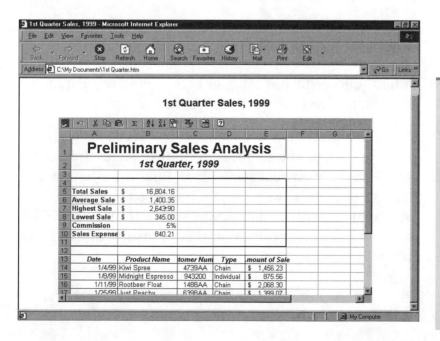

Using Web folders

To save a file on your Web server, click Web Folders in the shortcuts bar of the Save As dialog box. Next select the Web folder you want to use and click Save. To set up a Web server location as a Web folder, open Windows Explorer and click Web Folders. Next double-click Add Web Folder to work through a series of dialog boxes that help you specify the location as a folder.

Excel has embedded the codes necessary to view the worksheet with a Web browser, saved the worksheet file as 1st Quarter.htm in the location you specified, and handed control over to Internet Explorer. Viewers of this worksheet can scroll to see the hidden data. They can also use the buttons on the toolbar that spans the top of the worksheet to perform calculations, sort, and filter its data.

Viewing the HTML code

6. To see the underlying HTML coding, choose Source from Internet Explorer's View menu. Internet Explorer opens the 1st Quarter file in a separate Notepad window, like this:

```
1st Quarter - Notepad
File  Edit  Search  Help
<html xmlns:o="urn:schemas-microsoft-com:office:office"
xmlns:x="urn:schemas-microsoft-com:office:excel"
xmlns="-//W3C//DTD HTML 4.0//EN">

<head>
<meta http-equiv=Content-Type content="text/html; charset=windows-1252"
<meta name=ProgId content=FrontPage.Editor.Document>
<meta name=Generator content="Microsoft Excel 9">
<link rel=File-List href="./1st%20Quarter_files/filelist.xml">
<title>1st Quarter Sales, 1999</title>
</head>

<body>
<!--[if !excel]>  <![endif]-->
<!--The following information was generated by Microsoft Excel's Publis|
Page wizard.-->
<!--If the same item is republished from Excel, all information between
tags will be replaced.-->
<!---------------------------->
<!--START OF OUTPUT FROM EXCEL PUBLISH AS WEB PAGE WIZARD -->
<!---------------------------->

<div id="1999 Sales_2883" align=center x:publishsource="Excel">
```

Scary, isn't it?

7. In turn, click Notepad's Close button, Internet Explorer's Close button, and finally, Excel's Close button.

If your organization uses an intranet or a Web site to distribute information, you might want to take some time to explore Excel's Web publishing capabilities more thoroughly. Because you can always bring a published worksheet back into Excel for further editing, you may well find that HTML worksheets are a more dynamic way of distributing data that changes frequently than printing it on paper.

"Round-trip" editing

TWO

BUILDING PROFICIENCY

In Part Two, you build on the basic skills you developed in Part One. After finishing these chapters, you'll be able to design and implement many types of worksheets that help you manipulate and analyze information. In Chapter 4, you learn how to turn worksheet data into various kinds of graphs. In Chapter 5, you work with a database (known in Excel as a list) and create a pivot table. Finally, in Chapter 6, you conclude this Quick Course by tackling a series of more advanced techniques. You perform calculations on linked worksheets and use several types of what-if analysis.

4

Graphing Worksheet Data

You use Microsoft Graph to plot the data in an Excel worksheet as a graph so that you can analyze its components visually. Then you learn how to format the graph in a variety of ways, and finally, you preview and print the graph.

In this chapter, you create a graph using the worksheet of sales information, but you can easily apply these techniques to other types of data, such as student grades, competition scores, or scientific measurements.

Graph created and concepts covered:

Print the graph and its underlying worksheet on one page

Instantly format a worksheet with an autoformat

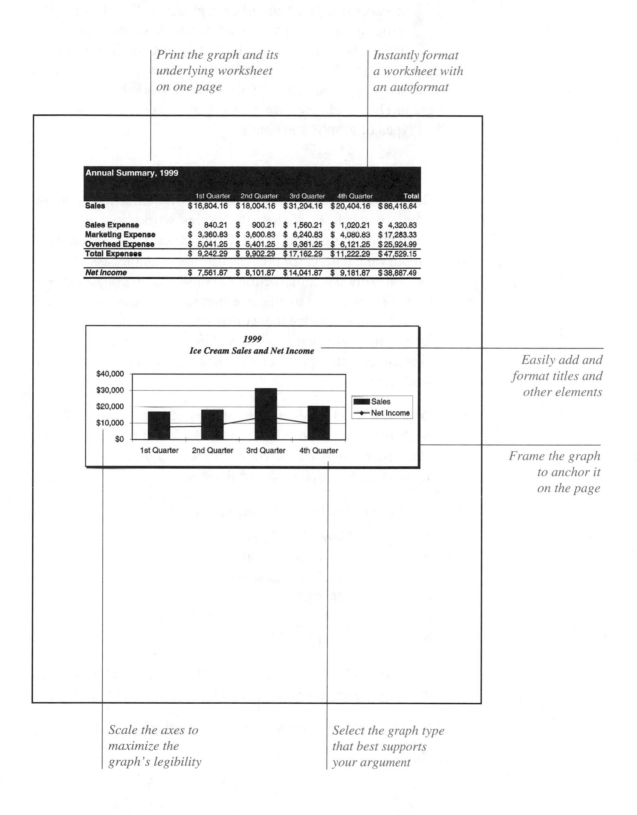

Annual Summary, 1999

	1st Quarter	2nd Quarter	3rd Quarter	4th Quarter	Total
Sales	$16,804.16	$18,004.16	$31,204.16	$20,404.16	$86,416.64
Sales Expense	$ 840.21	$ 900.21	$ 1,560.21	$ 1,020.21	$ 4,320.83
Marketing Expense	$ 3,360.83	$ 3,600.83	$ 6,240.83	$ 4,080.83	$17,283.33
Overhead Expense	$ 5,041.25	$ 5,401.25	$ 9,361.25	$ 6,121.25	$25,924.99
Total Expenses	$ 9,242.29	$ 9,902.29	$17,162.29	$11,222.29	$47,529.15
Net Income	$ 7,561.87	$ 8,101.87	$14,041.87	$ 9,181.87	$38,887.49

Easily add and format titles and other elements

Frame the graph to anchor it on the page

Scale the axes to maximize the graph's legibility

Select the graph type that best supports your argument

I n Part One, you learned enough about Excel to put the program to use in your own work. After all that effort, let's relax a bit in this chapter. Using the Totals worksheet of the 1999 Sales workbook as a basis, you'll explore various ways you can visually present worksheet data as a graph. (In this chapter, we use the generic term *graph* to mean all types of graphs and charts.)

Setting Up the Worksheet

Before you can start, you need to add some information to the Totals worksheet of the 1999 Sales workbook you have created for the Cream of the Crop ice cream company. To simplify the data-entry process for this example, assume that the company has a marketing expense that averages 20 percent of sales and an overhead expense (fixed costs) that averages 30 percent. Once the worksheet is in place, you can plot its information as various kinds of graphs. Assuming that you have already started Excel, follow these steps to complete the worksheet:

1. Open the 1999 Sales workbook, select row 5 of the Totals worksheet, and choose Rows from the Insert menu to insert a blank row. Then select rows 7 through 9 and choose Rows again to insert three more blank ones.

2. Enter the following information in the indicated cells:

A7	*Marketing Expense*
A8	*Overhead Expense*
A9	*Total Expenses*
B7	*=B4*0.2*
B8	*=B4*0.3*
B9	*=B6+B7+B8*

3. Select B7:B9 and drag the fill handle to copy the formulas in the range to the equivalent cells in columns C, D, and E.

4. Next select F6 and then drag the fill handle to copy its formula to F7:F9.

5. Select cell A11, replace Gross Profit with *Net Income*, and press Tab. Then enter *=B4-B9* in cell B11, and copy this formula to C11:F11.

6. Finally, widen column A so that all its labels are visible. The Totals worksheet now looks like this:

	A	B	C	D	E	F	G
1	**Annual Summary, 1999**						
2							
3		1st Quarter	2nd Quarter	3rd Quarter	4th Quarter	Total	
4	Sales	$ 16,804.16	$ 10,004.16	$ 31,204.16	$ 20,404.16	$ 86,416.64	
5							
6	Sales Expense	$ 840.21	$ 900.21	$ 1,560.21	$ 1,020.21	$ 4,320.83	
7	Marketing Expense	$ 3,360.83	$ 3,600.83	$ 6,240.83	$ 4,080.83	$ 17,283.33	
8	Overhead Expense	$ 5,041.25	$ 5,401.25	$ 9,361.25	$ 6,121.25	$ 25,924.99	
9	Total Expenses	$ 9,242.29	$ 9,902.29	$ 17,162.29	$ 11,222.29	$ 47,529.15	
10							
11	Net Income	$ 7,561.87	$ 8,101.87	$ 14,041.87	$ 9,181.87	$ 38,887.49	
12							
13							

Automatic Formatting

You have seen that you can use combinations of fonts and styles to draw attention to important worksheet details. Now let's look at a powerful Excel feature designed to make short work of worksheet formatting: *autoformats*. An autoformat is a predefined combination of formatting that works well with worksheets like the one you just created to produce fancy-looking reports with the click of a button. Try this:

Autoformats

1. Select A1:F11 and choose AutoFormat from the Format menu. Excel displays this dialog box:

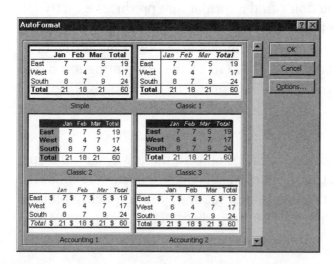

2. In the list box, find and select 3D Effects 1, click OK, and then click anywhere outside the table. Here's the impressive result:

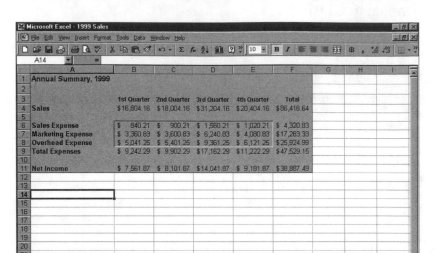

3. If you want, click the Print button to print the sales data so that you can admire the worksheet on paper.

4. Select A1:F11 again and choose AutoFormat from the Format menu. Select Colorful 2 from the list box and click OK to produce another eye-catching report.

5. Try some of the other autoformats, finishing with Classic 2.

The autoformats that come with Excel don't work well unless you set up your worksheet with them in mind. Nevertheless, they are a great way to become familiar with the many effects you can create with combinations of fonts, lines, colors, and shading. If you don't find a format that produces exactly the look you want, you can assign an autoformat as a starting point and then make refinements using the Font, Fill Color, Font Color, and Borders buttons on the Formatting toolbar or the options available in the Format Cells dialog box.

Plotting Graphs

With Excel, you can create graphs in three ways: on the current worksheet, as a separate sheet in the current workbook, or in another workbook. In this section, you'll quickly plot the sales data on the current worksheet. The advantage of this method is that you can then print the graph and the underlying

Removing worksheet autoformats

If you decide not to use a worksheet autoformat after all, select the formatted range, choose AutoFormat from the Format menu, select None from the list, and click OK.

worksheet on the same page. When you create a graph in Excel, a graphing program called Microsoft Graph actually does all the work. (Graph ships with Excel and is installed when you perform a Typical installation.) Here, you'll use Graph together with the Chart Wizard to create a few graphs. Don't be concerned if your graphs don't look exactly the same as ours. Differences in screen setup or the order of selecting functions can change the way graphs are displayed.

Microsoft Graph

When you create a graph from a selected range of data in a worksheet, Excel maintains a link between the worksheet and the graph. This link is dynamic: If you make changes to the worksheet data, Graph revises the graph to reflect the new data. You can create more than one graph from the same range of data, and the data can be arranged either in columns or rows.

The first graph you'll create is a column-oriented graph. Follow these steps:

1. Select A6:E8 on the Totals worksheet and click the Chart Wizard button on the Standard toolbar's More Buttons palette. You see the first of four dialog boxes that will now lead you through the process of creating and customizing a graph:

The Chart Wizard button

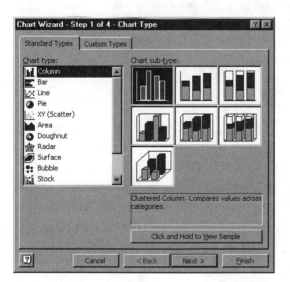

2. If necessary, click the Office Assistant's No option to decline its help. With Column selected in the Chart Type list, select

Clustered 3-D Column as the sub-type (the first option in the second row) and click Next to display this dialog box:

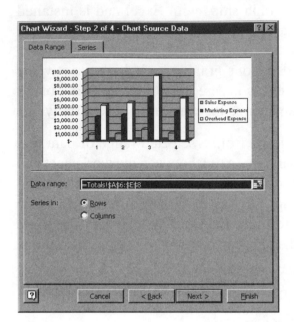

The Chart Wizard shows how the selected range will look as a 3-D column graph, with all labels and other information in place.

3. Click Next again to move to the next dialog box:

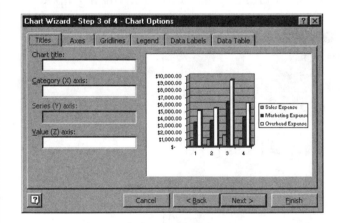

Creating graphs on chart sheets

To create a graph on a separate chart sheet, simply build the graph in the Chart Wizard's dialog boxes as usual and then select the As New Sheet option in the fourth Chart Wizard dialog box. In the adjacent edit box, you can type in a name for the new sheet or leave it as the default, *Chart1*. When you are done, click Finish; Excel inserts a chart sheet in front of the worksheet that is active and plots the graph on the new sheet. To quickly build a graph in the default format on a separate chart sheet, simply select the worksheet data you want to plot and press the F11 key.

At any point in the graph-creating process, you can click the Back button to move back to a previous dialog box so that you can change its settings.

4. Click each of the tabs of this dialog box to get familiar with the options. Then click Next to accept the default settings and move to the dialog box shown on the facing page.

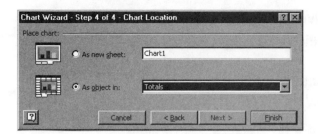

5. Here, the Chart Wizard asks where you want the graph to be displayed. With the As Object In option selected and Totals in the edit box, click Finish. Graph plots the graph and displays the Chart toolbar, as shown here:

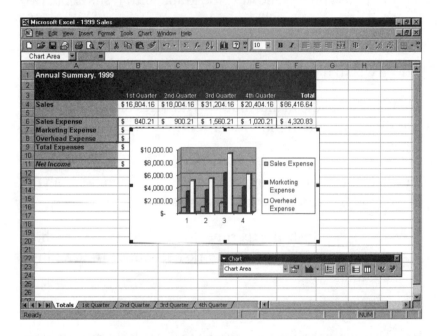

As you can see, four groups of columns represent the four quarters of expense data. Within each group, three colors represent the three expense categories, which are identified in the legend by the three labels from column A of the selected range: Sales Expense, Marketing Expense, and Overhead Expense. The graph is surrounded by small black squares, called *handles*, to indicated that it is selected. As long as the graph is selected, the Microsoft Graph program modifies the menus on the menu bar to accommodate the commands appropriate for working with graphs.

Handles

6. Click the Chart toolbar's Close button to turn it off.

Sizing and Moving Graphs

When Graph finishes plotting your data and places the graph on the worksheet, the program rarely places it where you want it to be. Fortunately, moving and sizing graphs is easy, and you can always drag the graph to the desired location and then adjust its size by dragging the handles around the graph's frame. Try this:

1. Move the mouse pointer over the graph near its outer edge.

ChartTips →

2. When a pop-up box that says *Chart Area* appears, hold down the left mouse button and drag the graph until it sits about two rows below the table. (The handy pop-up boxes that identify different elements of the graph are called *ChartTips*.)

Now try resizing the graph:

1. Point to the handle in the middle of the right side of the frame and drag it to the right. Graph redraws the graph within a wider frame.

Changing the height and width proportionally →

2. Drag a corner handle diagonally outward to increase both the height and the width proportionally.

3. When you've finished experimenting, reshape the graph so that it occupies an area of the worksheet about 16 rows high by 6 columns wide.

Updating Graphs

Excel has actively linked the graph to its underlying data, so if you change the data, Graph automatically redraws the graph to reflect the change. Try this:

1. Activate the 3rd Quarter worksheet and change the value in cell E14 to *$102,656.23*.

2. Return to the Totals worksheet. The formulas have gone to work, showing big changes in the expenses and net income.

3. Widen the columns of the worksheet so that you can see the recalculated values, and then check the result in the graph on the facing page.

Adding values to an existing series

If you add values to a set of data in your worksheet and want to update a graph you created earlier to reflect the new values, you can select the values and simply drag the selection to the graph. When you release the mouse button, Excel adds the additional data points along the category axis. To add values to a graph located on a separate chart sheet, you can select the values, click the Copy button, move to the chart sheet, select the graph, and click the Paste button.

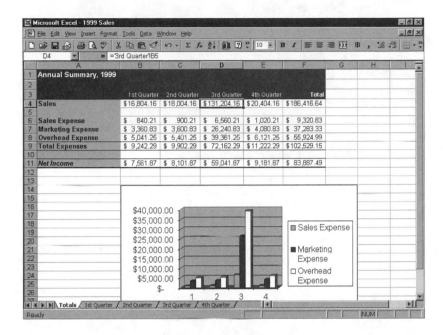

Graph has automatically adjusted the scale of the values to accommodate the unusually large expenses for the 3rd quarter.

4. Move back to the 3rd Quarter worksheet, click the arrow to the right of the Undo button, and select Typing "102656.23" In E14. This restores the original 3rd quarter amount on this worksheet and undoes the column adjustments on the Totals worksheet.

Changing the Graph Type

Let's plot a new graph from the quarterly sales data so that you can explore the available graphing possibilities. You'll start by deleting the current graph and creating a new one:

1. Move to the Totals worksheet, click the chart area to select the graph, and press the Delete key. Excel removes the graph from the worksheet.

Deleting graphs

2. Press Ctrl+Home and select A3:E4. The first row in this range contains labels that identify the four quarters of the year, and the second row contains numeric sales data.

3. Click the Chart Wizard button and click Finish to accept all the default settings in the four Chart Wizard dialog boxes.

Creating a default graph

4. After Graph draws the graph, move and resize it so it looks like the one shown on the next page.

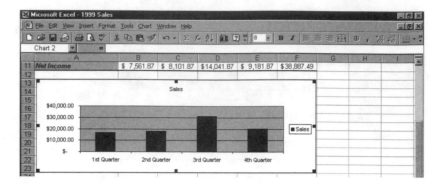

5. If the graph is not selected (surrounded by handles), click it.

6. Choose Chart Type from the Chart menu to display this dialog box:

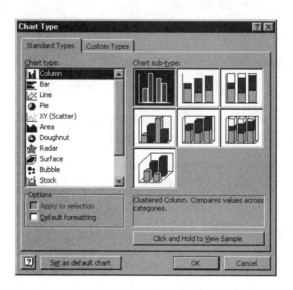

7. From the Chart Type list, select the Pie option and click OK. Graph draws this graph, in which the four quarters of sales data are represented as colored wedges in a circular pie:

Graph scale

If you change the source data radically, the scale of the entire graph might change. For example, if you enter an ice cream sales amount in the millions in the 1999 Budget, the other columns shrink to almost nothing to keep the scale consistent.

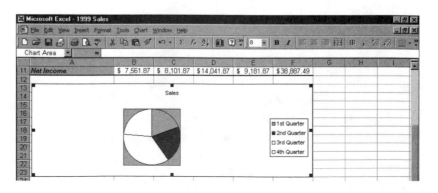

8. Point to each slice of pie in turn and wait until ChartTips tells you the slice's value and percentage.

Before taking a look at some of the other available types, let's simplify things a bit by enlisting the aid of the Chart toolbar. Then you'll add another set of data (the net income amounts) to the graph. Follow these steps:

1. Choose Toolbars and then Chart from the View menu to display the Chart toolbar. (Remember, you can move the floating toolbar out of the way by dragging its title bar, or you can "dock" it at the top of the window by double-clicking the title bar. See page 22 for more information.)

Displaying toolbars

2. Click the arrow to the right of the Chart Type button on the Chart toolbar to see this drop-down palette of graph types:

The Chart Type button

3. Click the Column Chart option (the third option in the first column) to restore the previous chart type.

4. Next click outside the graph to deselect it, select A11:E11 in the budget worksheet, and click the Copy button.

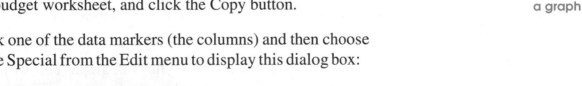

Adding a set of data to a graph

5. Click one of the data markers (the columns) and then choose Paste Special from the Edit menu to display this dialog box:

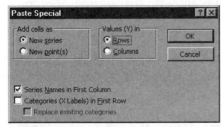

6. The default settings are correct, so click OK. Excel adds a second series of data markers to the graph, as shown on the next page.

Selecting graph objects

If you find selecting a graph object with the mouse difficult, you can select the object from the Chart Objects list at the left end of the Chart toolbar. Graph then places handles around the object so that you can format it in the usual way.

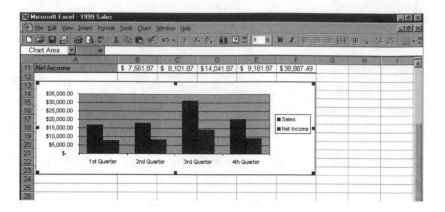

You can now compare sales with after-expenses income for each of the four quarters.

Types of graphs

No matter what type of graph you need—bar, pie, line, and so on—Graph has a format that will probably do the job. The available types include:

- **Column graphs.** The default format. Perfect for showing the variations in the value of an item over time, as with the budget example. In addition to the simple column graph that you've already created, you can plot stacked or 100-percent stacked column graphs; see the sub-types in the Chart Type dialog box shown on page 98.

- **Bar graphs.** Ideal for showing the variations in the value of an item over time, or for displaying the values of several items at a single point in time.

- **Line graphs.** Often used to show variations in the value of more than one item over time.

- **Area graphs.** Look something like line graphs but plot multiple data series as cumulative layers with different colors, patterns, or shades.

- **Pie graphs.** Ideal for showing the percentages of an item that can be assigned to the item's components. (Pie graphs can represent only one data series.)

- **Doughnut graphs.** Display the data in the shape of a doughnut. Similar to pie graphs, but they can display more than one data series.

- **XY (or scatter) graphs.** Used to detect correlations between independent items (such as a person's height and weight).

- **Radar graphs.** Plot each series on its own axis radiating from a center point.

- **High-low-close graphs.** Typically used to plot stock market activity.

In addition, you can create three-dimensional area, bar, column, line, pie, and surface graphs. And you can create various kinds of combination graphs, which plot one type of graph on top of another as an "overlay." Each type has several variations that will satisfy most of your graphing needs. Let's try changing the type of the graph currently on the screen so that you can see some of the possibilities:

3-D graphs

Combination graphs

1. Be sure the graph is selected. Then click the arrow to the right of the Chart Type button on the Chart toolbar and click the Line Chart button in the left column of the drop-down palette. Sales and net income are now represented as two separate lines on the graph, as shown here:

The Line Chart button

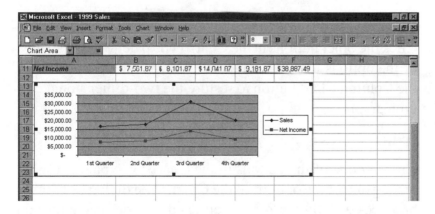

2. Display the Chart Type drop-down palette and click the 3-D Pie Chart button. Now the four quarters of sales data are represented as colored wedges in a circular pie with the illusion of three dimensions. You no longer see the net income data because a pie graph can display only one set of data, as shown on the next page.

The 3-D Pie Chart button

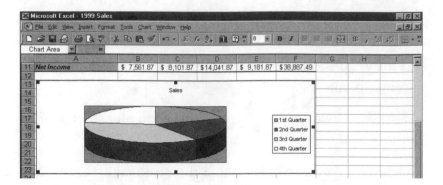

3. Finally, click the Doughnut Chart button in the Chart Type button's palette. The resulting graph displays two circles, one for each type of data:

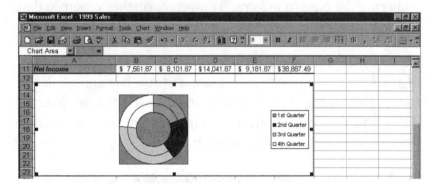

4. Click the other buttons in the Chart Type palette to get an idea of the options that are available. Then finish up by clicking the Column Chart button to restore the two-dimensional column graph.

Using Graph Custom Types

Clicking one of the buttons in the Chart Type palette (or selecting one of the options in the Chart Type dialog box) often produces exactly the graph you need, but occasionally you might want something slightly different. Before you spend time adjusting the format of a graph type, you should check out the sub-types displayed on the Custom Types tab of the Chart Type dialog box. Follow these steps:

1. With the graph selected, choose Chart Type from the Chart menu and click the Custom Types tab to display the options shown at the top of the facing page.

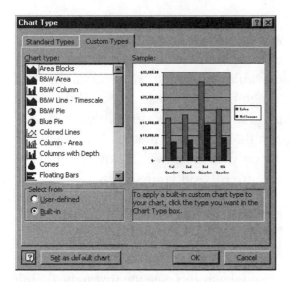

2. Scroll through the list, clicking any Chart Type options that catch your eye and noting their effect in the Sample box on the right.

3. When you've finished exploring, select Line-Column and click OK. The result—an example of a combination graph— is shown here:

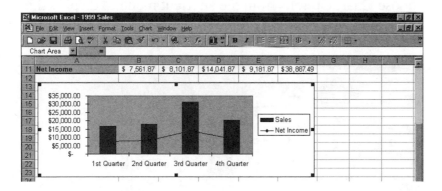

Fine-Tuning Graphs

As we have said, Graph has a graph type for almost every occasion. But often you'll want to refine the presentation of a graph by adding or changing specific elements. For this purpose, Graph provides a wealth of options for fine-tuning graphs. In the following sections, you'll use some of these options to add a title, adjust the value-axis labels, add a frame, and change gridlines. These elements increase almost any graph's clarity and persuasiveness.

X-axis and y-axis

Graph uses the terms x-axis and y-axis with some of its graph commands. For clarification, here are a couple of definitions: The x-axis shows the information categories, for example, sales and expenses; the y-axis shows the data points (plotted values).

You can use commands on menus to change the various elements of a graph; however, Graph provides shortcut menus to make the job of customizing even easier. Shortcut menus exist for almost every conceivable graph element. You might want to get a feel for the range of customization possibilities by right-clicking various graph elements (gridlines, axes, series, and so on) to open their shortcut menus. When you've finished experimenting on your own, we'll show you how to add a title to the graph currently on your screen.

Adding and Formatting Text

To dress up the graph, you can add a title with a subtitle and explanatory notes. (Titles appear at the top of the graph; notes can be placed anywhere on the graph. See the tip on the facing page.) You can also customize the axis labels. All the fonts and attributes available for worksheet entries are available for graph text, so you can format the text any way you want. Follow these steps to add a title to the graph:

Adding a title →

1. With the graph selected, point to the chart area (use ChartTips to make sure you're in the right place) and right-click. Then choose Chart Options from the shortcut menu to display this dialog box:

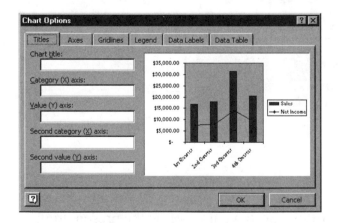

Displaying a data table

If you create a column, bar, line, or area graph on its own chart sheet or if the data used to plot the graph is not easy to spot on the worksheet, you can display a data table below the graph. Simply click the graph to select it, choose Chart Options from the Chart menu, and click the Data Table tab. Next click the Show Data Table check box and then click OK. If you want, you can add legend keys to the data table and delete the legend. To hide a data table, simply deselect the Show Data Table check box.

As you can see from the options, you can create a title and attach text to the axes.

2. Click an insertion point in the Chart Title edit box, type *1999*, and click OK.

3. Now click an insertion point at the end of the title, press Enter, and type *Ice Cream Sales and Net Income*. Then click anywhere on the graph to complete entry of the title, which now looks like this:

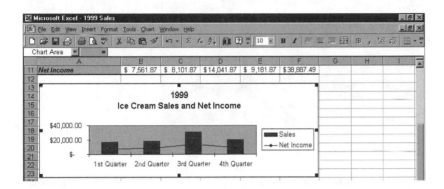

4. Right-click 1999 to display the title's shortcut menu. Then choose Format Chart Title and click the Font tab to display these options:

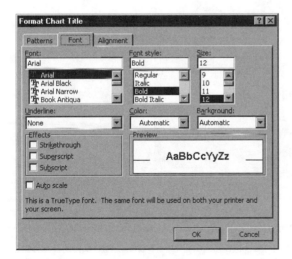

5. Select Times New Roman from the Font list, click Bold Italic in the Font Style list, and click OK.

Now let's make the default value-axis labels easier to read:

1. Right-click the value-axis numbers, choose Format Axis from the shortcut menu, and click the Number tab to display the dialog box shown on the next page.

Formatting the title

Adding notes

To add some explanatory notes to a graph, check that no graph element is selected, click an insertion point in the formula bar, type the note, and press Enter. Excel displays a text box containing the note in the middle of the graph. You can use the frame and handles surrounding the text box to reposition it and resize it. To format the text box and the note it contains, simply right-click the box, choose Format Text Box, and then make your selections in the dialog box.

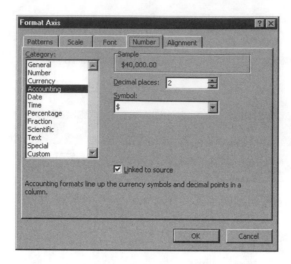

2. Select Currency as the category, change the Decimal Places setting to 0, and click the Scale tab to display these options:

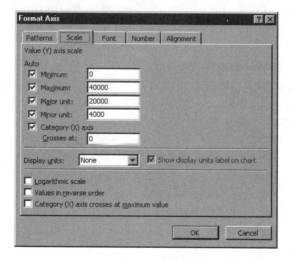

Creating graphics

With Excel's drawing tools, located on the Drawing toolbar, you can draw attention to specific parts of a graph or worksheet. For example, you might circle a data point or mark it with an arrow. You can even create simple graphics, such as a logo. Use the Line, Arrow, Rectangle, and Oval buttons to create a graphic object by clicking one of the buttons and dragging it over the graph or worksheet. Use the AutoShapes button to create even more objects, including flowchart shapes. Use the color and style buttons to adjust the object's line thickness, fill color, and pattern. To add free-floating notes to a graph or worksheet, click the Text Box button, drag to create a box, and type the note. To add fancy-lettered text, click the Insert WordArt button.

3. Under Auto, double-click the Major Unit edit box, type *10000* to display more labels along the value axis, and click OK. The results are shown here:

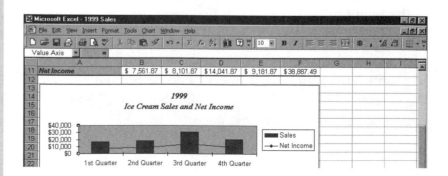

Enhancing the Graph's Border

You can use the Color and Font Color buttons on the Formatting toolbar to select colors and patterns for different elements of your graphs and worksheets. However, using the Format command on the shortcut menu is the quickest way to customize the graph's border. Try this:

1. If necessary, select the graph. Then right-click the chart area and choose Format Chart Area from the shortcut menu to display this dialog box:

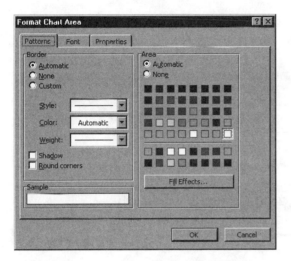

2. On the Patterns tab, click the arrow to the right of the Weight edit box in the Border section and select the third line in the drop-down list. Click the Shadow check box and then click OK.

You can also use this dialog box to give the graph's background a color or pattern.

Adding Gridlines

When gridlines would make it easier to read the plotted data, you can easily add them to a graph. You can also add lines for major or minor intervals on either or both axes. Your graph currently has no gridlines. Let's add them to the value axis to make it easier to identify the dollar amount of each marker:

1. With the graph selected, right-click any area of it. Choose Chart Options from the shortcut menu, and then click the Gridlines tab to display the dialog box shown on the next page.

Formatting legends

By default, Graph places the legend to the right of the plot area. If you want, you can move the legend to another part of the screen by simply dragging it. Alternatively, you can choose Format Legend from the legend's shortcut menu and select an option on the Placement tab in the Format Legend dialog box. Other tabs in this dialog box allow you to change the pattern, color, and font of the legend.

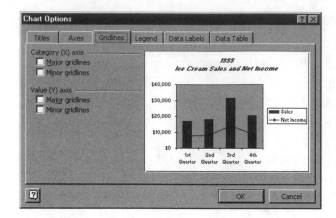

2. Click Major Gridlines in the Value (Y) Axis section. Then click OK. The graph now looks like this:

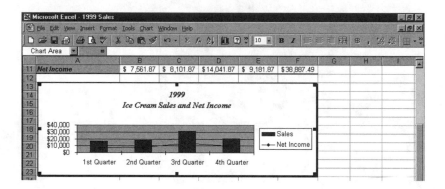

3. Click anywhere on the worksheet to deselect the graph and remove the Chart toolbar. Then save the workbook before moving on.

We won't take these customization experiments any further but will leave you to explore on your own. When you're ready, rejoin us to print the graph.

Previewing and Printing Graphs

Previewing and printing graphs is much like previewing and printing worksheets. You can preview and print the worksheet data and graph together or just the graph. Follow these steps:

1. Press Ctrl+Home and then click the Print Preview button. Your screen now looks as shown on the facing page.

Formatting data markers

To change the color, pattern, or legend name for a series of data markers, right-click any marker and then choose Format Data Series from the shortcut menu. Graph displays a dialog box in which you can make these and other types of changes to the markers.

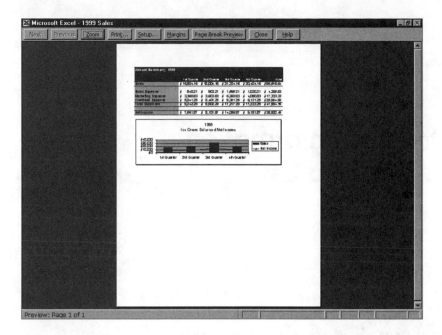

As you can see, one or two adjustments would greatly improve the look of this page.

2. Click the Close button to return to the worksheet.

3. Adjust the position of the graph so that it is separated from the worksheet entries by about five rows of blank cells, and adjust its size so that it is about 15 rows high.

4. Deselect the graph and click the Print Preview button again. Then on the Print Preview toolbar, click the Setup button.

5. Click the Margins tab and change the Top margin to *1.5*. In the Center On Page section, select the Horizontally option and then click OK.

6. If you want, click the Print button on the Print Preview toolbar to create a paper copy of the graph, which now looks as shown on page 89. Then click Close and save the workbook.

Now that you are acquainted with Microsoft Graph and its customization options, you are well-equipped to produce professional-looking worksheets and to give your audiences alternative, easy-to-grasp ways of viewing your data.

5

Extracting Information from a List

In Excel, a list is a simple database. Our examples show you how to sort data and use powerful, yet efficient tools to extract and manipulate information. You also experiment with filtering records, summarizing data, and creating a pivot table.

The techniques you learn here will help you work with any Excel database. You can use a pivot table to summarize any data, whether you are dealing with money, statistics, or measurements.

Worksheets created and concepts covered:

Create a pivot table to summarize worksheet data

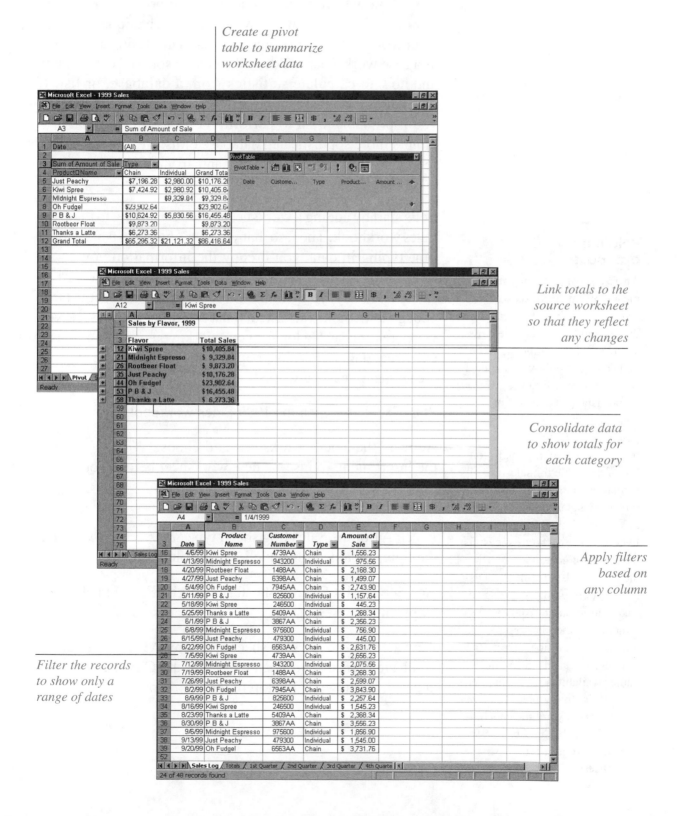

Link totals to the source worksheet so that they reflect any changes

Consolidate data to show totals for each category

Apply filters based on any column

Filter the records to show only a range of dates

You've covered a lot of important ground, and you now have a feel for some of the power of Excel. In this chapter, we show you more techniques for efficient worksheet creation and management. Using a sales log as a base worksheet, we describe how to sort and extract data and how to calculate statistics from a database, or list. If you have a database program, such as Microsoft Access, you'll probably want to perform these tasks using that program's more sophisticated database tools. But if your data is relatively straightforward, you can carry out many database tasks with Excel.

Let's start by adding a worksheet called Sales Log to the 1999 Sales workbook. Then, so that you don't have to spend a lot of time typing in data, you'll copy the information you've already entered in other worksheets to simulate a record of sales. That way, you will have a ready-made list that is large enough to demonstrate Excel's list-handling features. (If you were creating such a log for your work, you would obviously enter real data rather than copying it.) Follow these steps to create the Sales Log worksheet:

1. Start Excel and open the 1999 Sales workbook.

2. Activate the Totals worksheet and choose Worksheet from the Insert menu to insert a new worksheet before Totals.

3. Rename the new worksheet as *Sales Log*.

4. In cell A1 of the Sales Log sheet, type *Sales Log, 1999*, click the Enter button, and then click the Bold button.

5. Activate the 1st Quarter sheet, select A13:E25, and click the Copy button.

6. Activate the 2nd Quarter sheet and copy A14:E25. Because you have copied more than one item, the Clipboard toolbar appears, as shown at the top of the facing page.

Relational vs. flat databases

An Excel list is a flat database, meaning that it consists of one stand-alone table. You can sort the list, pull out specific records, and otherwise manipulate it, but you can work only with the data stored in that one table. A relational database consists of several tables that are linked by key fields. For example, a database for Cream of the Crop might consist of one table for sales-rep information, another for customer information, another for inventory, and another for invoices. Each invoice in the invoices table could be generated by using the key fields to pull the customer's billing, shipping, and tax status information from the customer table; the sales rep's name and phone number from the sales-rep table; and the product's name, availability, and unit price from the inventory table. This type of power is beyond the capabilities of Excel but is a breeze for database programs like Microsoft Access.

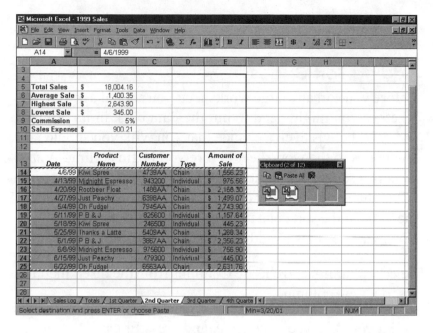

7. Repeat step 6 for the 3rd Quarter and 4th Quarter sheets.

8. Now activate Sales Log, select cell A3, and click the Paste All button on the Clipboard toolbar. Then after Excel pastes all four items from the Office Clipboard into consecutive ranges in the Sales Log sheet, close the Clipboard toolbar.

The Paste All button

9. Adjust the column widths so that all the entries are visible.

10. Press Ctrl+Home and then scroll through the worksheet. Notice that the IF function that calculated the category of sale has been replaced by its results. For purposes of this worksheet, this function is no longer needed, but if you want to retain the formulas, you should copy and paste each item separately.

The Sales Log worksheet now contains 48 rows of sales data, which is perfect for demonstrating some of Excel's list capabilities.

Sorting Data

The data in the quarter worksheets is not much larger than one screen. To find out which chain-store customer has purchased the most ice cream, you could simply look at the worksheet. Getting that information from the Sales Log worksheet is a little more difficult. Fortunately, Excel can quickly sort worksheets like this one, using up to three levels of sorting.

Adding Sort Codes

Before you sort any large worksheet, you should ask yourself whether you might need to put the data back in its original order. If there is even a chance that you will, you should add sort codes to the worksheet before you begin sorting. A *sort code* is a sequential number assigned to each row of entries. After changing the order of the entries, you can sort again on the basis of the sort code to put everything back where it was. Follow these steps to add sort codes to the sales log:

1. Select column A and choose Columns from the Insert menu to insert a new column.

2. Select cell A3, type *Sort Code*, and press Enter.

Creating a series of numbers →

3. In cell A4, type *1* and click the Enter button.

4. Hold down the Ctrl key and drag the fill handle in the bottom right corner of the selected cell down to cell A51. Excel uses the default settings of the Fill/Series command—Columns as the Series In option, Linear as the Type option, and a Step Value of 1 (see the adjacent tip)—to produce a sequential set of numbers in the selected range, as shown here:

A step value other than 1

To use AutoFill to create a series with a step value other than 1, enter the first and second values in the series, select both values, and drag the fill handle through the range in which you want the series to appear. The second value tells Excel what to use as a step value. For example, entering *1* and *4* tells Excel to create a series with a step value of 3—the difference between 1 and 4. (To create a series of numbers using AutoFill, you must enter two values; if you enter only one, Excel simply fills the range with the starting value.)

	Sort Code	Date	Product Name	Customer Number	Type	Amount of Sale
4	1	1/4/99	Kiwi Spree	4739AA	Chain	$ 1,456.23
5	2	1/8/99	Midnight Espresso	943200	Individual	$ 875.56
6	3	1/11/99	Rootbeer Float	1488AA	Chain	$ 2,068.30
7	4	1/25/99	Just Peachy	6398AA	Chain	$ 1,399.07
8	5	2/2/99	Oh Fudge!	7945AA	Chain	$ 2,643.90
9	6	2/8/99	P B & J	825600	Individual	$ 1,057.64
10	7	2/15/99	Kiwi Spree	246500	Individual	$ 345.23
11	8	3/1/99	Thanks a Latte	5409AA	Chain	$ 1,168.34
12	9	3/11/99	P B & J	3867AA	Chain	$ 2,256.23
13	10	3/15/99	Midnight Espresso	975600	Individual	$ 656.90
14	11	3/22/99	Just Peachy	479300	Chain	$ 345.00
15	12	3/29/99	Oh Fudge!	6563AA	Chain	$ 2,531.76
16	13	4/6/99	Kiwi Spree	4739AA	Chain	$ 1,556.23
17	14	4/13/99	Midnight Espresso	943200	Individual	$ 975.56
18	15	4/20/99	Rootbeer Float	1488AA	Chain	$ 2,168.30
19	16	4/27/99	Just Peachy	6398AA	Chain	$ 1,499.07
20	17	5/4/99	Oh Fudge!	7945AA	Chain	$ 2,743.90
21	18	5/11/99	P B & J	825600	Individual	$ 1,157.64
22	19	5/18/99	Kiwi Spree	246500	Individual	$ 445.23
23	20	5/25/99	Thanks a Latte	5409AA	Chain	$ 1,268.34
24	21	6/1/99	P B & J	3867AA	Chain	$ 2,356.23
25	22	6/8/99	Midnight Espresso	975600	Individual	$ 756.90
26	23	6/15/99	Just Peachy	479300	Individual	$ 445.00
27	24	6/22/99	Oh Fudge!	6563AA	Chain	$ 2,631.76
28	25	7/5/99	Kiwi Spree	4739AA	Chain	$ 2,656.23

Now let's look at various ways you might want to sort the Sales Log worksheet.

Using One Sort Column

The simplest sorting procedure is based on only one column. You indicate which column Excel should use, and the program rearranges the rows of the selected range accordingly. Let's start by sorting the data in Sales Log by customer type to see how the process works:

1. Select A3:F51.

2. Choose Sort from the Data menu. Excel displays the Sort dialog box:

You can select three different columns for sorting. Excel automatically enters the first column in the selection in the Sort By edit box.

3. You want Excel to use the Type column as the basis for a one-column sort. Click the arrow to the right of the Sort By edit box to drop down a list of the columns in the selection, and select Type.

    Specifying the column

4. By default, Excel selects Ascending as the sort order for the records. Click OK to sort the records with the current settings.

    Specifying the sort order

    The sales data is now sorted alphabetically by customer type, with all the sales to chain stores coming before those to individually owned stores.

Using Two Sort Columns

Now let's take things a step further and sort the sales data not only by type but also by product name:

1. With the range still highlighted, choose Sort from the Data menu. The previous sort column, Type, is still entered in the Sort By edit box.

2. To add a second sort column, click the arrow to the right of the first Then By edit box, select Product Name, and then click OK. (The square box between Product and Name is the line break that you inserted to make the column heading wrap within its cell. When you select Product Name, Excel enters only the word Product in the Then By edit box. This has no effect on the command's operation, but if this behavior makes you nervous, you can always reformat the column headings so that they appear on one line, and then adjust the column widths as necessary.)

The sales log is now sorted alphabetically by customer type and alphabetically within type by the product names of the ice cream.

Using Three Sort Columns

Depending on the focus of your current analysis, you might want to sort Sales Log based on the Date or Customer Number columns. However, let's assume you are interested in the sales volume of each product; therefore, you need to add one more column to the sort. Follow these steps to sort by type, product name, and amount of sale:

1. With A3:F51 still selected, choose Sort from the Data menu. Again, the Sort dialog box retains the selections from the previous sort.

2. Click the arrow to the right of the second Then By edit box, select Amount of Sale, and click OK.

3. Press Ctrl+Home to see the results, which are shown at the top of the facing page.

Sorting buttons

Two sorting buttons, located on the Standard toolbar, can be used when you are sorting data based on only one column. Tell Excel which column to use as the sort column by clicking a cell in that column before using the sorting button. Then click the Sort Ascending button to sort the list starting with A (or lowest digit) or the Sort Descending button to sort starting with Z (or highest digit). Excel then sorts the list based on the column containing the cell you selected. To restore the data to its original order, use the Undo button on the Standard toolbar.

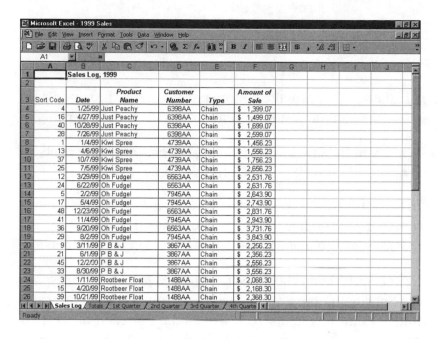

Keeping Headings in View

You can now scroll through the sales log to check how Excel has sorted the data, but as you scroll, the column headings will scroll out of sight. You can keep the headings at the top of the screen like this:

1. Scroll the worksheet so that row 3—the row with the column headings—is at the top of your screen.

2. Select cell A4 and choose Split from the Window menu to position a horizontal split bar across the worksheet window above the selected cell, like this:

Splitting a window horizontally

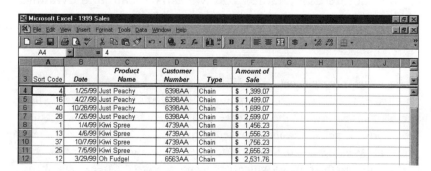

If you select any cell in row 1 (except A1) and choose Split, Excel positions a vertical split bar down the worksheet window to the left of the selected cell. If you select a single cell

Splitting a window vertically

that is not in row 1 or column A and then choose Split, Excel splits the window horizontally and vertically above and to the left of the selected cell.

3. Use the scroll bar for the bottom pane to scroll the sorted data while the column headings remain visible in the top pane.

Removing the split

4. When you finish viewing the data, restore the single pane by choosing Remove Split from the Window menu.

In the next sections, we'll cover Excel's list capabilities. First, however, follow these steps to restore the sales log to its original order and to make a few other necessary adjustments:

Restoring the original order

1. Select A3:F51 and choose Sort from the Data menu to display the Sort dialog box. Then click the arrow to the right of the Sort By edit box and select Sort Code. For each of the two Then By edit boxes, click their arrows and select (none) from their drop-down lists. Click OK. Excel sorts the records back into their original order.

2. Right-click the column A header to display the column shortcut menu and choose Delete. The sales log now contains only its original five columns.

List Basics

Lists

The sales log is an organized collection of information about ice cream sales. By common definition, it is a *database*, known in Excel as a *list*. A list is a table of related data with a rigid structure that enables you to easily locate and evaluate

---

Synchronized scrolling

If you split the worksheet window horizontally and then scroll the window by using the horizontal scroll bar, both panes of the window scroll so that columns always align. Likewise, if you split the worksheet window vertically and then use the vertical scroll bar, the rows scroll simultaneously.

Freezing panes

You can use Freeze Panes on the Window menu to lock rows, columns, or both so that you can then keep column or row headings in view while you scroll other portions of the worksheet. To freeze a row or rows, select the row above which you want to make the freeze and choose Freeze Panes from the Window menu. Similarly, to freeze a column or columns, select the column to the right of which you want to make the freeze and then choose the command. Selecting a single cell and then choosing the command freezes the rows above and columns to the left of the selected cell. Choose Unfreeze Panes to return the panes to their original condition.

individual items of information. Each row of a list is a *record* 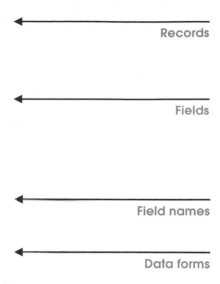 that contains all the pertinent information about one component of the list. For example, row 4 of the sales log contains all the information about one particular sale. Each cell of the list is a *field* that contains one item of information. Cell E4, for example, contains the amount of sale for the record in row 4. All the fields in a particular column contain the same kind of information about their respective records. For example, column A of the sales log contains the dates of all the sales. At the top of each column is a heading, called a *field name*.

Records

Fields

Field names

You perform Excel's list operations with the aid of a dialog box called a *data form*. As you'll see in the following sections, the options in the data form provide ways to find, add, delete, and modify records. Here's how to display the data form:

Data forms

1. Select the first cell of the list—in this case, cell A4.

2. Choose Form from the Data menu. The data form shown below appears:

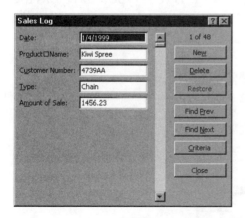

As you can see, the name of the sheet appears in the title bar of the dialog box. The column headings have become the field names and are displayed down the left side of the form. One record's data is displayed in the edit boxes adjacent to the field names. (If a field contains a formula, the data form displays the results of the formula, not the formula itself, and you can't edit the results in this dialog box.)

Data form size

Excel can display up to 32 fields on a data form. If your list has over 32 fields, when you choose Form from the Data menu to display a data form, Excel tells you that your list has too many fields. Reduce the number of fields and try again. (A quick way to reduce the number of fields without losing data is to insert a blank column after the 32nd field.)

Finding Records

The data form allows you to find records by stepping through the list one record at a time or by entering criteria to identify specific records. Let's step through the list first:

Displaying records
sequentially

1. Click the Find Next button in the data form. Excel now displays the second record. The numbers in the top right corner show how many records are in the list and which record is currently displayed.

2. Click the Find Prev and Find Next buttons to step back and forth through the list. When you are finished, use the scroll bar to the right of the fields to return to record 1.

You use the Criteria button in the data form to find a specific record or records in the list, like this:

Searching for specific
records

1. Click the Criteria button to display the criteria form, which resembles a blank data form.

2. To find all sales over $2,000 for P B & J, type *P B & J* in the Product Name edit box and *>2000* in the Amount of Sale edit box, as shown here:

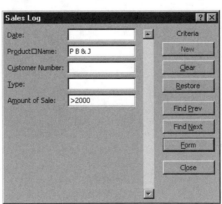

Comparison operators and wildcards

You can use these comparison operators to compute criteria:

= > < >= <= <>

and you can specify wildcards, using an * or a ? for matching text. For example, assuming another ice cream product named *Kiwi Jubilee* has been added to the list, you could specify *Kiwi** as the Product Name to locate the records for both Kiwi Spree and Kiwi Jubilee.

3. Click the Find Next button. Excel moves you back to the data form, where the first record in the list that meets the criteria is displayed. Click the Find Next button again, and Excel displays the next record that meets the criteria. You can continue clicking the Find Next button until you reach the end of the list. Then move back through the matching records by clicking the Find Prev button.

4. Return to the criteria form by clicking the Criteria button and then remove the criteria by clicking the Clear button.

Removing search criteria

5. Move back to the data form by clicking the Form button. All records are now accessible.

Adding and Deleting Records

The data form can be used to add and delete records from the list. As an example, you'll add a new record, find it, and then remove it from the list. Follow these steps:

1. With the data form displayed on your screen, click the New button. Excel clears the fields of the data form so that you can type the information for a new record. New Record is displayed in the top right corner.

Adding a new record

2. Fill in the record with the following data, using the Tab key to move from field to field:

Date	*11/4/99*
Product Name	*Rootbeer Float*
Customer Number	*4980AA*
Type	*Chain*
Amount of Sale	*1595*

The data form now looks like this:

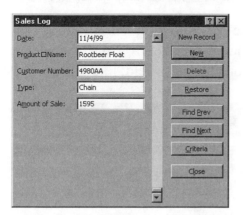

3. Click the New button or press Enter to add the record to the sales log. (Excel adds new records to the end of a list.)

4. Click the Find Prev button. Excel displays the record you just added—record 49.

The Restore button

When you are editing a record in a data form, you can restore the previous data by clicking the Restore button. This button works only if you haven't yet moved to another record or pressed the Enter key.

Deleting a record

5. With the new record still displayed, click the Delete button. Excel warns you that the record will be permanently deleted.

6. Click OK. Excel deletes the record and displays the data form for a new record.

7. Click the Find Prev button again. The last record in the list is again record 48.

8. Click Close to remove the data form from the screen and return to your worksheet.

Filtering Records

Suppose you have invested a considerable chunk of your advertising budget for the year on a direct-mail flyer about a two-week promotion. For another two-week promotion earlier in the year, you relied on your salespeople to get the word out to their customers. To assess which method is more effective, you want to compare sales during the two promotions. Or suppose you want to analyze all sales over $1,000 to see if you can detect sales patterns. In either case, you can tell Excel to extract all the relevant data for scrutiny. You give Excel instructions of this kind by choosing Filter and then AutoFilter from the Data menu and then defining filtering criteria. To see how AutoFilter works, try following the steps below:

Turning on AutoFilter

1. With row 3 displayed at the top of your screen and cell A4 selected, choose Filter and then AutoFilter from the Data menu. Excel displays arrow buttons for each field, like this:

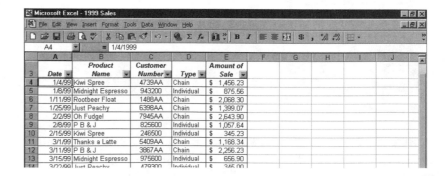

2. Click the arrow for the Type field. Excel displays a list of the unique values in the Type field (Chain and Individual) as well as three other options—All, Top 10, and Custom.

3. Click the arrow for the Product Name field. Again, Excel displays a list of the unique names in the field and the three other options.

4. Select Just Peachy. Excel immediately filters out all the applicable records, hiding the other records as shown here:

Notice that Excel retains the original record numbers and changes the color of the arrow for the Product Name field to indicate which column is being used for filtering.

Suppose you want to see the Just Peachy records for chain stores only. Try this:

1. Click the arrow for the Type field and select Chain. Now only the chain-store records for Just Peachy are displayed.

2. To display all of the Just Peachy records again, click the arrow for the Type field and select (All).

Customizing Filters

Now let's get a little fancy. Suppose you want to see only the records for Just Peachy with amounts over $1,000. To filter out these records, you use the Custom option on the drop-down list. Follow these steps:

1. Click the arrow for the Amount of Sale field and select (Custom...) to display the Custom AutoFilter dialog box shown on the next page.

Advanced filtering

You can create a criteria range on your worksheet to use for more complex filtering. For example, to find records over a certain amount for two products within a particular date range, you start by creating a three-column-by-three-row table, called a *criteria range*, above the list. In the first row, enter the Date, Amount of Sale, and Product Name field names, spelling them exactly as they are in the list. (Remove the line break from the Product Name field name in the list for filtering purposes.) In the second row, enter a specific date (or use comparison operators to enter a range), sales amount (preceded by >, the greater than symbol), and name of the first product. In the third row, enter the date, sales amount (preceded by >), and name of the second product. Then click any cell in the list and choose Filter and then Advanced Filter from the Data menu. Complete the dialog box by entering the references of both the list range and the criteria range (including both sets of field names), and click OK. Excel then extracts the requested data from the list. (Choose Filter and then Show All from the Data menu to restore the list.) Using a criteria range is especially useful if you want to extract records based on calculated criteria, because you can use Excel's functions in the criteria formulas.

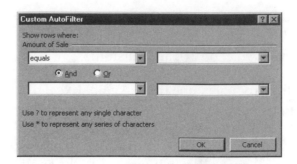

In this dialog box, you can use operators and the And or Or options to set criteria for the Amount of Sale field.

Using operators in filters

2. Click the arrow to the right of *equals* to display a list of operators, and then select *is greater than*.

3. Press the Tab key to move to the adjacent criteria box, and type *1000*.

4. Click OK. Excel selects the records and displays these results:

Removing filters

You can remove all the filters you've set up so far by choosing Filter and then Show All from the Data menu. You can then apply different filters to the entire list. As another example, let's filter out the second and third quarter sales from the list by using the Or option in the Custom AutoFilter dialog box:

Other AutoFilter options

When you select the Top 10 option from a column's drop-down list and set the Show options in the Top 10 AutoFilter dialog box, Excel sorts the rows based on the selected column and filters out the specified number of records at the top or bottom of the sorted list. For example, you can ask to see the eight records with the highest values in the Amount of Sale column.

1. Choose Filter and then Show All from the Data menu. Excel displays all the records in the database.

2. Click the arrow for the Date field and select (Custom...).

3. In the Custom AutoFilter dialog box, change the operator to *is greater than*, press Tab, and type *3/31/99* as the first criteria. Then with the And option selected, select *is less than* as the

operator, and type *10/1/99* as the second criteria. The dialog box looks like the one shown here:

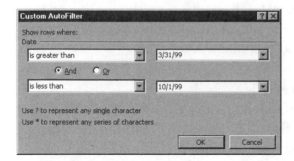

4. Click OK to display these results:

	A	B	C	D	E	F	G	H	I	J
3	Date	Product Name	Customer Number	Type	Amount of Sale					
16	4/6/99	Kiwi Spree	4739AA	Chain	$ 1,556.23					
17	4/13/99	Midnight Espresso	943200	Individual	$ 975.56					
18	4/20/99	Rootbeer Float	1488AA	Chain	$ 2,168.30					
19	4/27/99	Just Peachy	6398AA	Chain	$ 1,499.07					
20	5/4/99	Oh Fudge!	7945AA	Chain	$ 2,743.90					
21	5/11/99	P B & J	825600	Individual	$ 1,157.64					
22	5/18/99	Kiwi Spree	246500	Individual	$ 445.23					
23	5/25/99	Thanks a Latte	6409AA	Chain	$ 1,268.34					
24	6/1/99	P B & J	3867AA	Chain	$ 2,356.23					
25	6/8/99	Midnight Espresso	975600	Individual	$ 758.90					
26	6/15/99	Just Peachy	479300	Individual	$ 445.00					
27	6/22/99	Oh Fudge!	6563AA	Chain	$ 2,631.76					
28	7/5/99	Kiwi Spree	4739AA	Chain	$ 2,656.23					
29	7/12/99	Midnight Espresso	943200	Individual	$ 2,075.56					
30	7/19/99	Rootbeer Float	1488AA	Chain	$ 3,268.30					
31	7/26/99	Just Peachy	6398AA	Chain	$ 2,599.07					
32	8/2/99	Oh Fudge!	7945AA	Chain	$ 3,843.90					
33	8/9/99	P B & J	825600	Individual	$ 2,257.64					
34	8/16/99	Kiwi Spree	246500	Individual	$ 1,545.23					
35	8/23/99	Thanks a Latte	5409AA	Chain	$ 2,368.34					
36	8/30/99	P B & J	3867AA	Chain	$ 3,556.23					
37	9/6/99	Midnight Espresso	975600	Individual	$ 1,856.90					
38	9/13/99	Just Peachy	479300	Individual	$ 1,545.00					
39	9/20/99	Oh Fudge!	6563AA	Chain	$ 3,731.76					

Sales Log / Totals / 1st Quarter / 2nd Quarter / 3rd Quarter / 4th Quarter

24 of 48 records found

5. Turn off filtering by choosing Filter and then AutoFilter from the Data menu to toggle it off. Excel displays all the records and removes the arrows from the field names.

Turning off AutoFilter

By using filtering, you can act on only the filtered records, without affecting the other records in the database. For example, you can change the font of filtered records or sort them. You can also create a graph using the data from filtered records (see Chapter 4 for information about graphs).

Summarizing Data

Often you will want to summarize the data in a list in some way—for example, by totaling sets of entries. In this section, you'll first summarize data using a technique called *consolidation*, and then you'll create a *pivot table*.

Consolidating Data

Suppose you want to total the sales amounts on the Sales Log sheet by ice cream flavor, but instead of putting the totals on the same sheet, you want to enter them on a separate worksheet and create a link between the totals and their source data so that if the data changes, the totals will, too. This task seems pretty complicated, but it's simple with Excel. Follow the steps below:

1. So that the two columns of the Sales Log worksheet that you want to consolidate appear side-by-side, select column E and move it to column F, select column B and move it to column E, and finally, delete column B.

2. Insert a new worksheet between Totals and 1st Quarter and rename the sheet as *Flavor Totals*.

3. Enter the title *Sales by Flavor, 1999* in cell A1, enter *Flavor* in cell A3, and enter *Total Sales* in cell B3. Then make all the entries bold, and widen columns A and B to fit their entries.

4. Select cell A4 and choose Consolidate from the Data menu to display this dialog box:

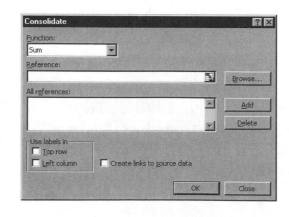

Consolidating data from multiple worksheets

To consolidate data from more than one worksheet, the data in each of the source worksheets must be arranged in the same way. For example, if customer names are in column B in Sheet1, they must also be in column B in Sheet2, Sheet3, Sheet4, and so on. Furthermore, all of the worksheets must contain the same customer names in the same order. After setting up a consolidation worksheet, select the destination area and choose Consolidate from the Data menu. Select a function (such as Sum), enter a reference to the first source worksheet, click Add, enter a reference to the second source worksheet, and so on. Then click OK. Excel performs the consolidation, assembling the data from the source worksheets in your consolidation worksheet.

5. If Sum does not already appear in the Function edit box, select it from the Function drop-down list.

6. Click an insertion point in the Reference box, and then click the Sales Log tab. Excel enters the name of that sheet.

7. Click the Collapse button at the right end of the Reference box, and if necessary drag the dialog box's title bar to move it out of the way. Then select D4:E51, and click the Expand button. Excel has entered an absolute reference to the selected range in the Reference box.

The Collapse and Expand buttons

8. In the Use Labels In section, select the Left Column option. Excel uses the entries in the Product Name column on the Sales Log sheet as labels on the Flavor Totals sheet. (Excel also redisplays the Flavor Totals sheet at this point.)

9. Select Create Links To Source Data to link the data in the Flavor Totals sheet to the data in the Sales Log sheet, and click OK to perform the consolidation. The results are shown here:

	A	B	C
1	Sales by Flavor, 1999		
2			
3	Flavor		Total Sales
12	Kiwi Spree		$10,405.84
21	Midnight Espresso		$ 9,329.84
26	Rootbeer Float		$ 9,873.20
35	Just Peachy		$10,176.28
44	Oh Fudge!		$23,902.64
53	P B & J		$16,455.48
58	Thanks a Latte		$ 6,273.36
59			

Excel has entered the product names as row headings in the Flavor column and has added the sales amounts for each flavor and entered the results in the Total Sales column. The program inserted a column and outlined the worksheet to hide the mechanisms used to maintain the link between the totals and their source data. (For more about outlining worksheets, see the adjacent tip.) Let's display the hidden information:

1. Click the small button with the plus sign to the left of the row 12 header to display the underlying data for the Kiwi Spree flavor. Then click the plus sign button to the left of the row 21 header to display the data for Midnight Espresso.

Outlining worksheets

Excel's outlining feature lets you view as little or as much of a worksheet as you want to see. To outline a worksheet, select all the cells containing data and choose Group And Outline and then Auto Outline from the Data menu. Excel searches for what it considers to be the most important information (for example, the totals) and then uses this information to create different row and column outline levels. Initially, an outlined worksheet displays all its levels. You use the row level buttons and column level buttons in the top left corner of the window to expand and collapse the outline. For example, clicking the 2 row level button displays only the first and second levels and hides any lower levels. You can also click the buttons marked with minus signs above and to the left of the worksheet to collapse an outline level. Excel deduces that the last row or column of a section is the "bottom line" of the collapsed section and displays only that row or column. Conversely, you can click the buttons marked with plus signs to expand collapsed levels. Choose Group And Outline and then Clear Outline to leave outline mode.

2. Now click the small button with the number 1 in the top left corner of the worksheet. All the underlying (second level) data disappears and only the consolidated (first level) data appears.

Recall that you created a link between the Sales Log sheet and the Flavor Totals sheet when you selected the Create Links To Source Data option in the Consolidate dialog box. To test the validity of that link, follow these steps:

1. Display the Sales Log sheet and change the entry in E4 to $10,000.

2. Now display the Flavor Totals sheet and check that the total sales amount for Kiwi Spree has changed from $10,405.84 to $18,949.61.

3. Before you continue on to the next section, redisplay the Sales Log sheet and restore the entry in cell E4 to $1,456.23. (You might want to check the Flavor Totals sheet again to be sure that it has been updated as well.)

Creating Pivot Tables and Pivot Charts

Excel's PivotTable And PivotChart Wizard walks you through the steps of creating a pivot table or pivot chart with the type of summary calculation you specify. After you create a pivot table, you can reformat it by "pivoting" rows and columns on the screen to provide different views of the data. If you also create a pivot chart, any reformatting is reflected in the chart, as well. In this section, you'll use the sales log to build a pivot table, and then you'll modify the table and use it to create a pivot chart:

1. Activate the Sales Log worksheet and select cell A4.

2. Choose PivotTable And PivotChart Report from the Data menu to display the first of the PivotTable And PivotChart Wizard's four dialog boxes, shown on the facing page. (If necessary, click the Office Assistant's No button.)

External data sources

You can create a pivot table using data from a file created outside of Excel, such as a database, text file, or the Internet. To use an external data source, click External Data Source in the PivotTable And PivotChart Wizard's first dialog box, click Next, and then click Get Data. (You may need to install Microsoft Query first.) Click OK to define a new data source. In the Create New Data Source dialog box, enter a name for the query and specify a driver which tells Excel what program the data source comes from. Then click Connect. Navigate to the file you want to use and click OK three times. Excel starts the Query Wizard to guide you through defining the data you want to use.

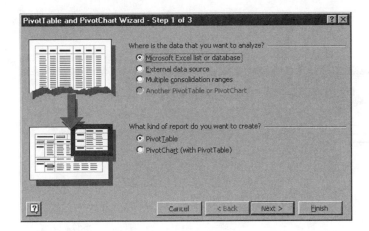

As you can see, you can use a single list that was created in Excel, a database that was created in a database program like Access or SQL (Structured English Query Language), or multiple ranges. You can create just a pivot table or a pivot table with a pivot chart. (You can't create a pivot chart by itself.)

3. Click Next to create a pivot table from an Excel list. The wizard displays this Step 2 dialog box:

4. Select the range A3:E51 and then click Next to display this Step 3 dialog box:

5. Click Finish. Excel inserts a new worksheet to the left of Sales Log and displays the PivotTable toolbar.

Naming lists

If you know you will add data to a list for which you are constructing a pivot table, assign a name to the entire list and enter that name in the Range edit box of the Step 2 dialog box. Then any data you add will be included in future versions of the pivot table (after you click the Refresh Data button on the PivotTable toolbar) without requiring that you go back and adjust the range.

6. Rename the new worksheet as *Pivot*. Your screen now looks like this:

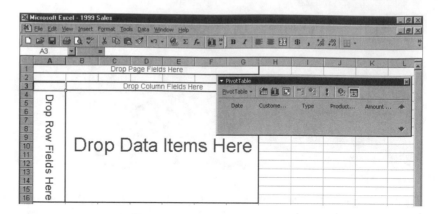

Now let's construct the pivot table directly on the worksheet by dragging the necessary fields, which are displayed on the toolbar as buttons, to the appropriate layout areas:

Building the pivot table

1. Point to Product on the toolbar. ScreenTips displays the entire field's name and tells you to drag it to the pivot table.

2. Drag the Product Name field button to the row area, drag the Type field button to the column area, and then drag the Amount of Sale field button to the data area. Here are the results:

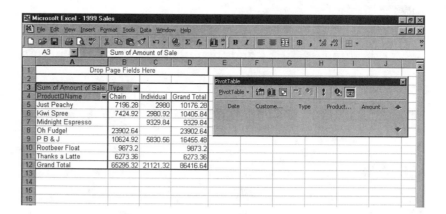

Excel has totaled the sales by product and by type, and has also calculated totals for each product and type.

As you can see, the Product Name and Type fields have arrows that are similar in appearance and function to those that appear in filters. Follow these steps to see how they work:

1. Click the arrow to the right of Product Name to drop down a list of products.

Filtering in a pivot table

2. Deselect the check boxes of all the flavors except Midnight Espresso and Oh Fudge! and click OK to see these results:

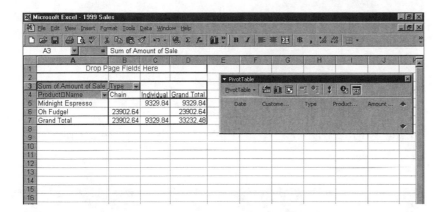

The pivot table clearly shows that, for some reason, individually owned ice cream stores are buying a lot of Midnight Espresso and no Oh Fudge! while chain stores are buying a lot of Oh Fudge! and hardly any Midnight Espresso.

3. Click the Product Name arrow again, reselect all the flavors, and click OK.

Modifying a Pivot Table

Now that you have built a basic table, you can easily modify it. Let's try changing the table in a couple of ways:

1. Drag the Date field button from the PivotTable toolbar to the page area, which gives you another way to filter the data in the table. (The filter is currently set to All dates.)

2. Click the filter's arrow and select any date from the drop-down list to display the totals for that day. The results are not very exciting for this sales log, but you can see the potential for daily, weekly, monthly, or quarterly analysis of real data.

3. Return the date setting to All.

Follow the steps on the next page to change the type of calculation for the Amount of Sale field by using the Field Settings button.

Updating pivot tables

If you change the data in a list that is the source for a pivot table, you can update it to reflect the new data by first clicking any cell in the pivot table and then clicking the Refresh Data button on the PivotTable toolbar or by choosing the Refresh Data command from the Data menu.

The Field Settings button

1. Select cell A3, which contains Sum Of Amount Of Sale, and click the Field Settings button on the PivotTable toolbar to display this dialog box:

2. In the Summarize By list, select Count and click OK. The pivot table now looks like this:

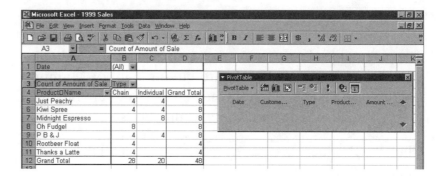

3. To total the sales again, click the Field Settings button and select Sum from the Summarize By list; don't click OK yet.

Formatting a pivot table

4. To format the values in the pivot table, click the Number button to display the Format Cells dialog box, select the Currency category, and click OK twice. Excel totals the sales by product and by type of store, displays the results in dollars and cents, and adjusts the column widths to accommodate the new values, as shown here:

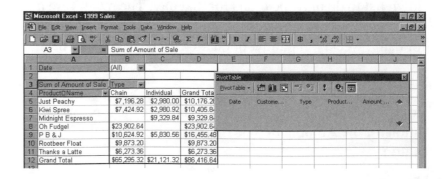

Plotting the Pivot Table as a Pivot Chart

You can easily get a visual representation of the data in a pivot table by plotting the data. Here's how:

1. On the PivotTable toolbar, click the Chart Wizard button. The wizard instantly plots the data in the pivot table as a column chart on a new worksheet, and it opens the Chart toolbar. Your screen now looks like this (we've docked the Pivot-Table and Chart toolbars on the right side of the window):

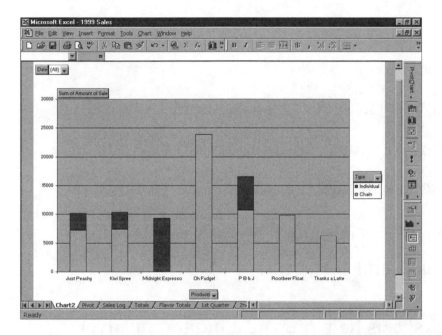

2. Click the Type arrow, deselect the Individual check box, and then click OK.

3. Now click the arrow to the right of the Chart Type button on the Chart toolbar and click the Pie Chart button. Instantly the chart is redrawn to visually identify each ice cream flavor's contribution to chain store sales.

4. Save and close the workbook.

In this chapter, we've barely scratched the surface as far as pivot tables in particular and lists in general are concerned. As you use these features, you'll find that they can make light work of extraction and summarization, perhaps encouraging you to tackle tasks that would otherwise seem too intimidating, cumbersome, or time-consuming.

6 More Advanced Calculations

You build a set of worksheets and link them so that the formulas in one worksheet can look up information in another. You also use iteration to project profit margin. Then we cover three types of what-if analysis: goal-seeking, data tables, and scenarios.

Our sample worksheets help prepare a bid for an advertising project. They can easily be adapted to estimate the costs of any type of project or event, such as an in-house training seminar or a fund-raising dinner.

Worksheets created and concepts covered:

Resolve circular references with iteration

Look up information in other workbooks

Create scenarios to evaluate the effect of changes

Use the Goal Seek command to find an unknown value

Use data tables to calculate the effects of one or two variables

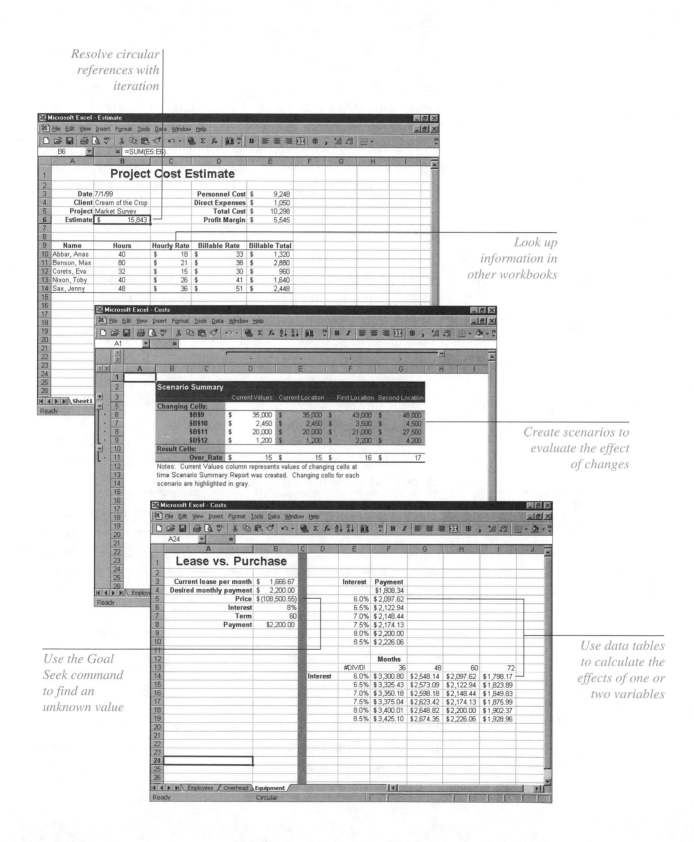

In this chapter, you tackle a more ambitious set of work-sheets and an advanced set of calculations. First you create tables of employee information and overhead costs. Then you create a worksheet in another workbook that estimates project costs by "looking up" hourly rates in one of the tables. Next we cover a technique called *iteration*, which enables Excel to resolve circular calculations. Finally, you explore some of Excel's tools for "what-if" analysis: the Goal Seek command, data tables, and Scenario Manager. For the exercises in this chapter, you'll develop worksheets for an advertising agency that wants to bid on a marketing-research project for the Cream of the Crop ice cream company.

Deciding what information you'll need

In our example, you create only employee information and overhead tables, because the primary cost involved in the project estimate is for people's time. However, you can easily adapt the project estimate worksheet to incorporate other types of expenses. For example, if you manage a construction business that specializes in bathroom and kitchen remodeling, you can create a table with up-to-date prices for fixtures, plumbing supplies, cabinets, tile, and so on, in addition to the employee information and overhead tables. Even if you are a one-person operation with no employees, you can still adapt the worksheet to make sure that you include overhead and other costs in your project estimates.

This chapter differs from previous chapters in that we don't bog down the instructions with information you already know. For example, we might show you a worksheet and ask you to create it without always telling you step by step what to enter, how to apply formats and styles, and how to adjust column widths. We leave it up to you to create the worksheet using the illustration as a guide. Similarly, we might tell you to create a formula, assuming that you know how to enter a function in a cell and how to click cells to use their references as arguments.

For this example, you'll organize the project information in two sheets, Employees and Overhead, saved within a single workbook. You'll also work with multiple workbooks and create links between them.

Creating the Supporting Tables

The logical way to begin this example is to enter the data needed for the two supporting tables. There's nothing complicated about these tables; we've stripped them down so that you don't have to type any extraneous information. The few calculations involved have been greatly simplified and do not reflect the gyrations accountants would go through to ensure to-the-penny accuracy. Instead of describing in detail how to create these tables, we'll simply show them to you and, after discussing the few formulas and cell and range names involved, let you create them on your own:

1. Open a new workbook, rename Sheet1 as *Employees*, and then save the workbook in the My Documents folder as *Costs*.

The Employees sheet

2. Create the following table of employee information:

3. In row 4, enter the formulas below and on the next page:

C4   =B4/50/30
          Annual salary divided by 50 weeks (allowing 2 weeks per year for vacation), divided by 30 billable hours per week (allowing 2 hours per day of nonbillable time)

D4   =B4*.22
          Employer contributions to social security and benefits estimated at 22 percent of annual salary

Ascending order

You can list employees in the employee information table in any order, but before Excel can use the table to look up information, you must sort it in ascending order. Excel cannot look up information in randomly ordered tables or in tables in descending order. Select the range and use the Sort command on the Data menu to sort the table (see page 115).

The ROUND function

E4	=D4/52/30
	Employer contributions to social security and benefits divided by 52 weeks divided by 30 hours per week
F4	=ROUNDUP(C4+E4,0)
	Salary per hour plus benefits per hour, rounded upward to a whole number

4. After entering the formulas in row 4, select C4:F13 and choose Fill and then Down from the Edit menu to copy the row 4 formulas to rows 5 through 13.

5. Adjust the column widths as needed to make the table more readable. Then use the Decrease Decimal button on the Formatting toolbar to display no decimals in the amounts in columns C and F.

6. Now add one more employee to the list. In cell A14, type *Wood, John*, press Tab, type *19000* and press Tab again. Excel automatically extends the formulas and formatting of C14:F14 into the cells below. Finish the record by selecting cell G14, typing *y*, and pressing Enter.

7. Assign the name *Billable* to cells G4:G15 and the name *Emp_Rate* to cells A4:F15. (See page 62 for information about how to assign range names.) You'll use these names in future formulas to create links between this and other worksheets. Press Ctrl+Home and save your work. Here is the completed table:

Extending named ranges

It is a good idea to always include a blank row or column at the end of a range when assigning range names. If you need to add employees to the Employees sheet, for example, you can select the blank row below the last entry and choose Rows from the Insert menu to add a new row. Because the blank row is part of the range named Billable, Excel automatically extends the range name definition to include the new row.

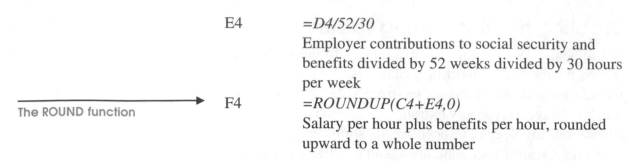

That's it for the employee information table. Let's move on to the overhead table:

1. Activate Sheet2, rename it as *Overhead*, and create the first part of the table shown here:

The Overhead sheet

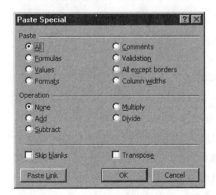

2. Don Funk and Wendy Vasse are officer/employees who do not directly generate income for the company, so you need to include their salaries and benefits in this overhead calculation. Activate the Employees worksheet, select A7:F7, click the Copy button, activate the Overhead worksheet, right-click cell A4, and choose Paste Special from the cell shortcut menu to display this dialog box:

3. Click the Paste Link button to insert links to Don Funk's information in the Employees worksheet.

4. Repeat steps 2 and 3 to insert links to Wendy Vasse's information. Then format the dollar amounts appropriately.

5. Next enter *Expenses/Hour* in cell E14 and *Total Billable Overhead/Hour* in cell E16. Make both entries right-aligned and bold, and preformat cells F14 and F6 as currency with no decimals. The worksheet looks like the one shown here:

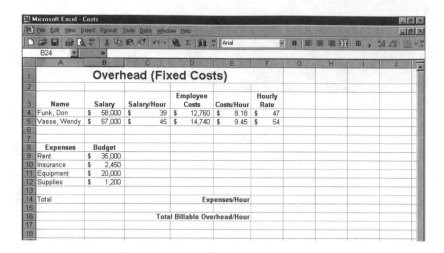

6. Now enter and format these formulas in the designated cells:

B14   =SUM(B9:B13)
F14   =ROUND(B14/52/30,0)
F16   =SUM(F4:F14)

You must bill 30 hours each week at the rate in F16 to cover overhead costs. You cannot bill overhead to a client directly, so you must increase the hourly rate of employees with billable hours by a prorated amount to ensure that overhead is included in project estimates.

Counting Entries

To calculate the prorated overhead amount, you need to divide the total billable rate per hour in cell F16 by the number of employees who generate income. You can glance at the Employees sheet and know that this number is 9, but what if the company had many employees? You can use the COUNTA function to tell Excel to count the number of employees who have a *y* entry in the Billable column of the Employees sheet. Excel then scans the range specified as the function's argument and counts the number of nonblank cells in the range. Here's how to use COUNTA in the formula that calculates the overhead allocation:

COUNTA vs. COUNT

Don't confuse the COUNTA function with the COUNT function. COUNTA tells you how many cells in the selected range contain entries of any sort, whereas COUNT tells you how many cells in the range contain numeric values.

1. In cell E17 in the Overhead sheet, enter *Prorated Overhead/ Hour* and make the entry bold and right-aligned.

2. You want the prorated amount to be in whole dollars, so you need to nest the prorated calculation in a ROUND function. Preformat cell F17 as currency with no decimals and then enter the following:

   =ROUND(F16/COUNTA(Billable),0)

   Excel calculates the formula and enters the result in cell F17, as shown here:

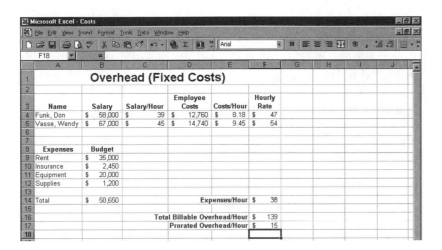

3. Assign the name *Over_Rate* to cell F17, and then save the workbook.

Creating an Estimate Worksheet

With the two tables in place, you're ready to create the worksheet for estimating project costs. You'll build this worksheet in a new workbook because the Costs workbook contains essential business information that might be needed in other types of calculations. If you isolate this type of information in its own workbook, you ensure that you don't have to go hunting for it each time you need it.

First you'll build the basic structure of the project estimate worksheet, and then you'll fill in the formulas necessary for the calculations. Follow the steps on the next page.

Listing names

Excel keeps track of the ranges to which you have applied a name. You can click a cell in a worksheet, press F3 to display the Paste Name dialog box, and then click the Paste List button to insert a list of range names with their references in the worksheet, starting at the selected cell. If you often assign names (and especially if you use multiple sheets within a workbook), this list can be useful in tracking the locations of the names in the workbook.

1. Click the New button on the Standard toolbar and then save the new workbook in the My Documents folder as *Estimate*. Now create the top area of the worksheet, as shown below:

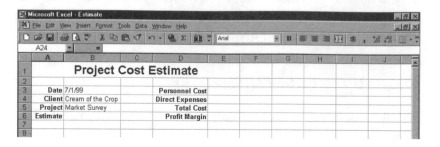

2. Next enter the headings in row 9 for the table where you'll calculate the personnel costs of the project. Enter the employee names and the number of hours you anticipate each will need to work on this project, as shown here:

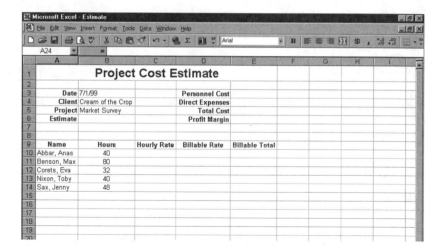

So far, everything has been pretty straightforward; these examples have given you an opportunity to practice skills you learned in other chapters but not much else. Now we'll introduce the Excel function that will enable you to use one of the tables you created earlier to fill in the information needed for this worksheet.

Looking Up Information

Excel has a variety of functions you can use in formulas to look up information in worksheet tables. Among them are

VLOOKUP (for vertically oriented tables) and HLOOKUP (for horizontally oriented tables). In this section, we'll show you how to use the VLOOKUP function. (See the tip on page 137 for details about sorting a table before you use Excel to look up information.)

Functions for looking up information

Excel needs three pieces of information to carry out the VLOOKUP function: the entry you want it to look up, the range of the lookup table, and the number of the column in the table from which the function should copy a value. You supply these three pieces of information in this way:

The VLOOKUP function

=VLOOKUP(Lookup_value,Table,Column_index)

Excel searches down the leftmost column of the lookup table for the row that contains the value you supply as the first argument. Then, if Excel finds the value, it looks along that row to the column you supply as the third argument, and the result of the VLOOKUP function is the value from the cell at the intersection of the row and column. Let's see how to put the VLOOKUP function to work:

1. In Sheet1 of the Estimate workbook, select cell C10 and click the Paste Function button. Then select Lookup & Reference in the Function Category list, select VLOOKUP in the Function Name list, and click OK to display this dialog box:

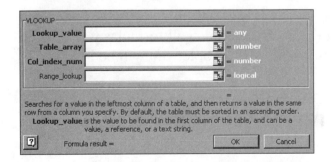

2. Click the Collapse button at the right end of the Lookup_value edit box, click cell A10 on the worksheet, and then click the Expand button.

Specifying the lookup value

3. Click the Table_array edit box, choose the Costs workbook from the bottom of the Window menu, and click the Employees tab (even if that sheet is already displayed). Then type

Specifying the lookup table

Emp_Rate. Excel enters a reference to the specified workbook, sheet, and range in the Table_array edit box. It also establishes a link between the Estimate and Costs workbooks by using the name of the Costs workbook in the formula it is building in the formula bar.

Specifying the lookup column

4. Click the Col_index_num edit box and type *6* to tell Excel to find the answer in the sixth column.

5. Click OK. Excel looks up the value in cell A10 (Abbar, Anas) in the lookup table named Emp_Rate on the Employees sheet of the Costs workbook, and it enters the corresponding hourly rate in cell C10 of Estimate, as shown here:

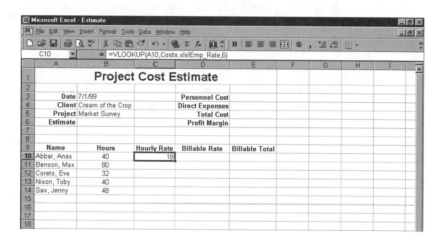

6. Now all you have to do is use AutoFill to copy the formula in cell C10 to C11:C14. Then equivalent formulas will look up the hourly rates for the other people who will be involved in this project.

Completing the Estimate

Well, the hard part is over. A few simple calculations, and you'll be ready to prepare an estimate for Cream of the Crop:

1. Enter the following formula in cell D10:

=*C10+Costs!Over_Rate*

Notice that you don't have to type the sheet name because it is part of the definition of the range name.

The Range_lookup argument

By default, the VLOOKUP function searches for the closest match to the Lookup_value argument you specify. If you want VLOOKUP to look for an exact match, simply enter =*FALSE* in the Range_lookup edit box to tell VLOOKUP that a "close enough" search won't meet your needs.

2. Next enter this formula in cell E10:

*=B10*D10*

3. Use AutoFill to copy the formulas to D11:E14.

4. Select C10:E14 and format the range as currency with no decimals. Then set off the table in A9:E14 with lines or borders. For example, we selected A9:E9 and used the Borders button to add lines above and below the headings, and then selected A14:E14 and added a line below the table. When you've finished, press Ctrl+Home to view the results:

Now you can calculate total costs in the summary area at the top of the worksheet:

1. Make these entries in the indicated cells:

E3	*=SUM(E10:E14)*
E4	*1050*
E5	*=E3+E4*

2. Format cell E4 as currency with no decimals. (The entry in this cell is an estimate of charges that will be incurred for long-distance phone calls, delivery services, and other expenses attributable directly to the project.)

Projecting Profit Margin with Iteration

Probably the most difficult part of estimating a project is figuring out the profit margin. You now have a good idea of what this project is going to cost. But suppose you need a

Easy opening of linked worksheets

When a worksheet contains a reference to a cell on a sheet in a different workbook, Excel asks if you want to reestablish the link to the cell when you open the worksheet. The linked workbook doesn't have to be open for this retrieval to take place, but if you want, you can open it by choosing the Links command from the Edit menu. Excel displays a dialog box listing all workbooks that are referred to by formulas in the active worksheet. Select the workbook you want to open and click the Open Source button.

margin of roughly 35 percent of the estimate total to be sure you make a profit. How do you calculate the actual profit margin when you don't yet know the estimate total, and how do you calculate the estimate total when you don't know the profit margin? You could go in circles forever.

Fortunately, you can have Excel go in circles for you. Using the iteration technique, you can force Excel to calculate the profit margin formula over and over until it can give you an answer. Follow the steps below:

1. Preformat cell E6 as currency with no decimals and then enter this formula:

   =0.35*B6

   The answer is nothing because B6 has no entry.

2. Next preformat cell B6 as currency with no decimals and enter this formula:

   =SUM(E5:E6)

When you enter the second formula, Excel tells you that it can't calculate the formula because of a circular reference. Here's why: The formula in B6 adds the values in E5 and E6. The formula in E6 multiplies the result of the formula in cell B6 by 35 percent. Excel cannot arrive at a result because when it adds E5 and E6, the formula in E6 must be recalculated; and as soon as Excel recalculates the formula, E6 changes, so E5 and E6 must be added again and so on, forever.

3. Click OK to close the message.

4. If this is the first time you've entered a circular reference, the Help window opens with the topic that explains circular references. Read the information and click the Close button. Excel then displays the Circular Reference toolbar and identifies the cells involved in the formulas with *tracer arrows*. Whether you see the Help window or not, the message *Circular: E6* appears in the status bar below the worksheet, telling you that the formula in E6 is the culprit.

Here's how to force Excel to come up with an answer:

Circular references

The Circular Reference toolbar

You can use the buttons on the Circular Reference toolbar to track down the components of a formula that involves a circular reference. Select a cell reference in the Navigate Circular Reference box and click the Trace Dependents button to see which cells use the selected cell in their formulas. Or click the Trace Precedents button to see which cells are used by the selected cell. The relationships are indicated on the worksheet by tracer arrows. You can remove the arrows by clicking the Remove All Arrows button. Then select another cell reference and repeat the tracking process.

1. If necessary, close the Circular Reference toolbar.

2. Choose Options from the Tools menu and click the Calculation tab. Excel displays the options shown here:

← Turning on Iteration

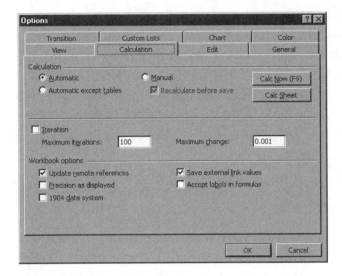

3. Select the Iteration check box and then click OK. You return to the worksheet, where Excel quickly recalculates the formulas, finally coming up with the results shown here:

Name	Hours	Hourly Rate	Billable Rate	Billable Total
Abbar, Anas	40	$ 18	$ 33	$ 1,320
Benson, Max	80	$ 21	$ 36	$ 2,880
Corets, Eva	32	$ 15	$ 30	$ 960
Nixon, Toby	40	$ 26	$ 41	$ 1,640
Sax, Jenny	48	$ 36	$ 51	$ 2,448

Project Cost Estimate

Date	7/1/99		Personnel Cost	$ 9,248
Client	Cream of the Crop		Direct Expenses	$ 1,050
Project	Market Survey		Total Cost	$ 10,298
Estimate	$ 15,843		Profit Margin	$ 5,545

Selecting the Iteration option tells Excel to ignore the circular reference and keep recalculating the formulas, going in circles. By default, Excel recalculates the formulas 100 times or until the values change by less than .001. The result produced by these settings is not exact, but in this example, the slight inaccuracy is not likely to cause concern. (You can increase

Types of calculation

By default, Excel immediately calculates a formula when you enter it and also recalculates any of the existing formulas in open worksheets that are affected by the new entry. To tell Excel to calculate open worksheets only when you press the F9 key, choose Options from the Tools menu, click the Calculation tab, and then select the Manual option. You might want to activate this option for large worksheets, where recalculating each formula can take some time.

the accuracy of the result by changing the Maximum Iterations or Maximum Change setting in the Options dialog box.)

What-If Analysis

The completed project estimate worksheet shows current employee and overhead costs. A number of factors could affect these costs in the future, which would in turn have an impact on the project estimate. In this section, we'll briefly look at three tools for assessing what that impact might be. (A fourth tool, the Solver, deals with multiple variables and constraints and is beyond the scope of this book. Check the Help feature for more information.)

Using Goal Seek to Find One Unknown Value

Goal Seek →

With Excel, you can use the Goal Seek command on the Tools menu when you know all of a function's arguments except one. As an example, suppose the market-research company is leasing equipment at a cost of $20,000 a year (see cell B11 of the Overhead sheet in the Costs workbook) with a negotiable option to buy the equipment. You want to calculate the purchase price that will allow you to buy the equipment without drastically increasing your overhead. Follow these steps:

1. Switch to the Costs workbook, activate Sheet3, and rename it as *Equipment*.

2. Set up the worksheet so that it looks like the one shown here:

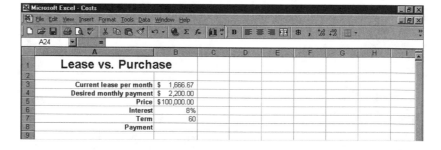

The PMT function →

3. Next enter a PMT function in cell B8 to calculate the loan payment using the trial values in B5:B7. Select cell B8, click the Paste Function button, click Financial in the Function Category list, click PMT in the Function Name list, and click OK.

4. In the Rate (for *interest rate*) edit box, type *B6/12* to specify the monthly interest rate.

5. In the Nper (for *number of periodic payments*) edit box, type *B7*, and in the Pv (for *present value of the amount borrowed*, or the price) edit box, type *B5*. Then click OK. Excel calculates the monthly payments for a 60-month (5-year) loan of $100,000 at 8% per year.

Now you'll use Excel's Goal Seek command to calculate the price you can afford to pay for the equipment if you want your monthly payment to be no more than $2,200 per month:

1. With cell B8 selected, choose Goal Seek from the Tools menu to display this dialog box, where Excel has entered a reference to the selected cell in the Set Cell edit box:

2. Type *2200* in the To Value edit box to tell Excel the maximum value allowed in the cell specified in the Set Cell edit box.

3. In the By Changing Cell edit box, click cell B5 to specify that this is the value Excel can play with to get the result you want. Then click OK. When Excel has finished its calculations, it displays a status box.

4. Click OK to close the box, and then widen column B to see the price Excel has entered in cell B5: $108,500.55. (See the adjacent tip to find out why Excel enters a negative number.)

Using Data Tables to Calculate the Effects of One or Two Variables

Now that you know approximately how much the market-research company can afford to pay to buy its leased equipment, let's look at the effect that rising or falling interest rates might have on your formula. You could make separate calculations

Negative payments

The PMT function takes into account money coming in and going out. If you borrow or buy something on credit, you enter a positive loan amount (or price), and the function displays a negative payment amount—the loan comes in and the payments go out. If you lend money, you enter a negative loan amount, and the function then displays a positive payment amount—the loan goes out and the payments come in.

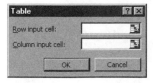

Data tables

The Fill Color button

for a range of interest rates, but Excel makes this sort of calculation easy with a tool called *data tables*. Here's how to set one up:

1. Separate the Goal Seek calculation from the data table by selecting column C, clicking the arrow to the right of the Fill Color button, and selecting any color except white. Then reduce the width of the column.

2. Set up columns E and F of the worksheet to look like the ones shown here (for aesthetic reasons, leave column D blank):

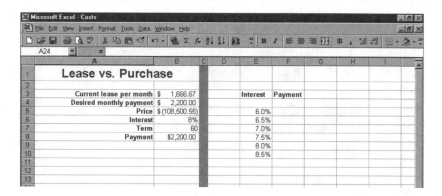

3. Now select cell F4 and enter the following PMT function, which tells Excel to calculate a monthly payment using the annual interest rate in cell E4 (converted to a monthly rate), the number of payments in cell B7, and the price in cell B5:

   =PMT(E4/12,B7,B5)

Arrays

If you look at any of the entries in cells F5:F10, you'll see that each result is calculated by the formula {=TABLE(,E4)}. These braces show that Excel is using an array for the calculation. The subject of arrays is beyond the scope of this book, but briefly, an array is a set of values used when calculating formulas that either take multiple values as one of their arguments or produce multiple values as their result.

Excel uses the formula's arguments to calculate the monthly payment. Because there is no interest rate in cell E4, Excel displays in cell F4 the result when the interest rate is 0% (you wish!). To tell Excel to transfer each of the interest rates in E5:E10 to E4 in turn (in effect, using cell E4 as a kind of scratchpad), you need to define the data table, like this:

4. Select E4:F10 and choose Table from the Data menu to display this dialog box:

5. Because the interest rates are arranged in a column, enter *E4* (the cell used as the PMT function's *rate* argument) in the Column Input Cell edit box and click OK. Excel calculates the PMT function for each of the rates in column E and displays the results in the adjacent cells in column F.

6. Format F4:F10 as currency and then take a look at the results.

Now let's quickly see how you would set up the data table to examine the effects of both a varying interest rate and a varying number of payments. Follow these steps:

1. Set up the cells below the first data table to look like this:

2. Enter the following PMT function in cell E13, the cell at the intersection of the column of rates and the row of monthly payments:

=PMT(D13/12,E12,B5)

Excel uses the specified interest rate (D13/12), number of payments (E12), and price (B5) to calculate the monthly payment. Because there is no interest rate in cell D13 and no number of payments in E12, Excel displays an error message in cell E13. To tell Excel to use the interest rates in E14:E19 and the number of payments in F13:I13, you again need to define the data table.

3. Select E13:I19 and choose Table from the Data menu.

Using a variable range in several formulas

You can use the same variable range to calculate more than one formula. For example, you could enter in cell G4 a second formula that also refers to the empty cell E4, select E4:G10, choose Table from the Data menu, enter a reference to cell E4 in the Column Input Cell edit box, and click OK. The results of the formula in cell F4 will appear in F5:F10, and the results of the formula in cell G4 will appear in G5:G10.

4. In the Row Input Cell edit box, enter *E12* because the numbers of payments are arranged in a row. In the Column Input Cell edit box, enter *D13* because the interest rates are arranged in a column. Then click OK. Excel calculates the PMT function for each of the rates in column E and the numbers of payments in row 13.

5. Format F14:I19 as currency. The results are displayed here:

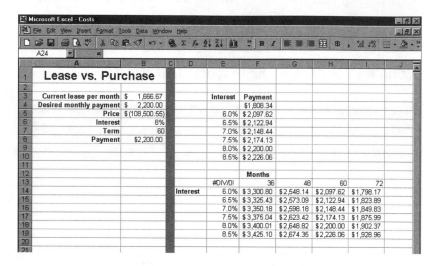

We've gone over data tables very quickly, and you might have trouble understanding them at first. If you want to explore further, check Excel's Help feature for more information.

Using Scenario Manager to Test Multiple Scenarios

Suppose the market-research company will be moving into a new facility next year and is looking at two possible locations. How will the move and an anticipated increase in project activity affect overhead costs and, therefore, project costs? You can use Excel's Scenario Manager to create multiple *scenarios* of the expense information so that you can analyze project costs before and after the move.

Scenario Manager

To demonstrate some of the capabilities of Scenario Manager, you'll assign the current nonemployee expenses of the overhead table to a scenario name and create two other scenarios for future nonemployee expenses. Then you'll change the scenarios to see the effect on project costs.

Creating Scenarios

Let's start by designating the expenses range in the Overhead sheet as the changing cells in the scenarios:

1. In the Costs workbook, activate the Overhead sheet, select B9:B12, and choose Scenarios from the Tools menu to display the Scenario Manager dialog box shown here:

2. Click the Add button to display this dialog box:

Adding the first scenario

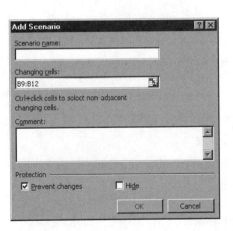

3. Type *Current Location* in the Scenario Name edit box and click OK to display the Scenario Values dialog box:

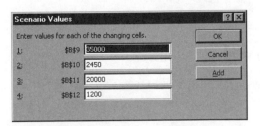

Adding a second scenario ──────▶ 4. The values displayed are those selected in the worksheet. Click Add to keep these values and add the second scenario.

5. Type *First Location* in the Scenario Name edit box and click OK to display the Scenario Values dialog box.

6. Change the values as shown here:

   1. $B$9   *43000*
   2. $B$10   *3500*
   3. $B$11   *21000*
   4. $B$12   *2200*

Adding a third scenario ──────▶ Then click Add again to keep these numbers and add the third scenario.

7. Type *Second Location* in the Scenario Name edit box and click OK.

8. Change the values as shown here:

   1. $B$9   *48000*
   2. $B$10   *4500*
   3. $B$11   *27500*
   4. $B$12   *4200*

   Then click OK to return to the Scenario Manager dialog box, which now looks like this:

Merging scenarios

You can create a worksheet with a scenario and send copies to colleagues to input their scenario values. When they return their copies, you can click the Merge button in the Scenario Manager dialog box, select their worksheets, and merge them into Scenario Manager. Then you can view and edit their scenarios or use them in summary reports.

9. Click Close to return to the workbook.

Changing Scenarios

By changing scenarios, you can display different versions of a worksheet to see the results of various conditions or assumptions. In the project estimate worksheet, you can use the scenarios you've created to show the effect of future overhead costs on project costs and profit margin.

To make it easier to access the scenarios and see their effects, you'll display the Costs and Estimate workbooks side by side. Follow the steps below to set up the screen:

1. Choose Arrange from the Window menu and click OK to accept the default Tiled option.

2. Scroll columns D and E into view in the Estimate window.

You are now ready to run the scenarios. Here's how:

1. To begin, activate the Costs workbook and choose Scenarios from the Tools menu. Then select First Location in the Scenarios list, click Show, and click Close. The expense cells change based on the values you defined for the First Location scenario, and Excel recalculates both workbooks, as shown below. (You may have to scroll the appropriate areas into view.)

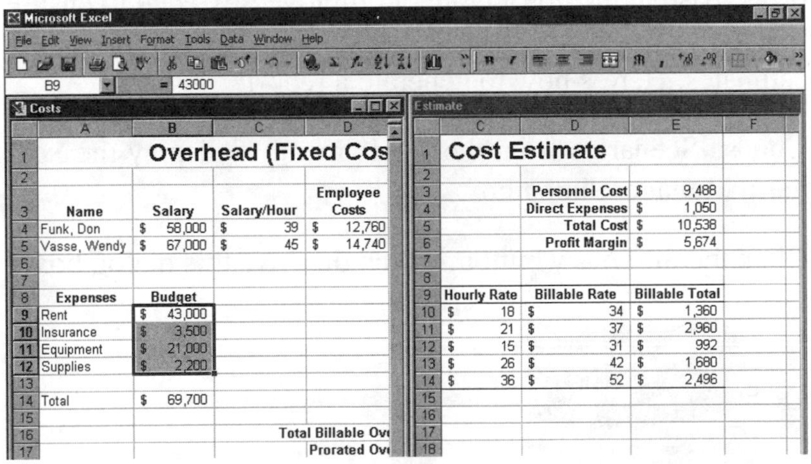

Selecting a scenario

2. Display the Scenario Manager dialog box again and select Second Location from the Scenarios list. Click Show and then Close to produce the results shown on the next page.

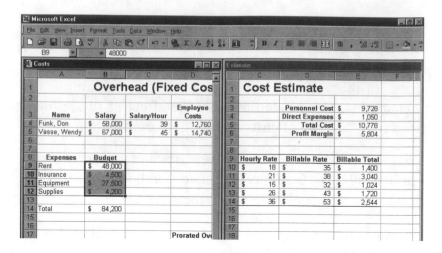

3. Return the expense cells to their original values by selecting Current Location from the Scenarios list in the Scenario Manager dialog box. Then maximize the Costs window.

Creating Scenario Reports

The Scenario Summary

Now that you have completed the building of the scenarios, let's use Scenario Manager to print a report. The Scenario Summary report displays the values of all the scenarios and their effects on the result cells. In this example, the result cell is the Prorated Overhead/Hour amount in cell F17 in the Overhead sheet of the Costs workbook. It shows the amount of increase in the hourly rate of employees needed to ensure that the increase in overhead is taken into account in project estimates. Here's how to generate a report:

1. Choose Scenarios from the Tools menu to display the Scenario Manager dialog box.

2. Click the Summary button, which displays this dialog box:

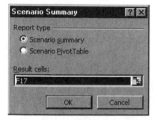

By default, Scenario Manager has selected the Scenario Summary option in the Report Type section and entered a reference to F17 in the Result Cells edit box.

3. Click OK. Scenario Manager creates a new sheet named Scenario Summary between the Employees and Overhead sheets in the Costs workbook and builds the report, like this:

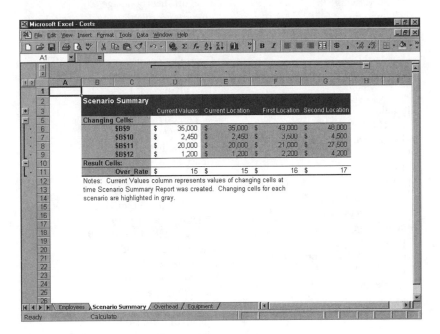

Scenario Manager displays the report in outline format so that you can easily hide or display rows and columns. (See the tip on page 127 for information about outlining worksheets.)

4. If you want a printed copy of the report, click the Print button. Then save and close both workbooks.

You now have a completed project estimate that takes into account the overhead costs as well as the direct costs associated with the market-research project. You also have a means of assessing the impact of varying overhead costs, and you can easily set up scenarios to examine the effects of other changes, such as salary increases.

As we said at the beginning of the chapter, you can adapt this set of worksheets in many ways to help you quickly assemble bids. You can also use versions of these worksheets for such tasks as comparing the cost of doing projects in-house with estimates that you receive from vendors. And once you have set up a lookup table such as the employee information table, you can link it to worksheets that perform a variety of other personnel-related calculations.

Index

Quick Course® Books

Offering beginning to intermediate training, Quick Course® books are updated regularly. For information about the most recent titles, call 1-800-854-3344 or e-mail us at quickcourse@otsiweb.com.

AVAILABLE QUICK COURSE®BOOKS		
1-58278-005-6	Quick Course® in Microsoft Access 2000	$14.95
1-879399-73-3	Quick Course® in Microsoft Access 97	$14.95
1-879399-52-0	Quick Course® in Microsoft Access 7	$14.95
1-879399-32-6	Quick Course® in Access 2	$14.95
1-58278-003-X	Quick Course® in Microsoft Excel 2000	$14.95
1-879399-71-7	Quick Course® in Microsoft Excel 97	$14.95
1-879399-51-2	Quick Course® in Microsoft Excel 7	$14.95
1-879399-28-8	Quick Course® in Excel 5	$14.95
1-58278-008-0	Quick Course® in Microsoft FrontPage 2000	$14.95
1-879399-91-1	Quick Course® in the Internet Using Microsoft Internet Explorer 5	$14.95
1-879399-68-7	Quick Course® in Microsoft Internet Explorer 4	$14.95
1-879399-67-9	Quick Course® in the Internet Using Netscape Navigator, ver. 2 & 3	$14.95
1-58278-001-3	Quick Course® in Microsoft Office 2000	$24.95
1-879399-69-5	Quick Course® in Microsoft Office 97	$24.95
1-879399-54-7	Quick Course® in Microsoft Office for Windows 95/NT	$24.95
1-879399-39-3	Quick Course® in Microsoft Office for Windows, ver. 4.3	$24.95
1-58278-006-4	Quick Course® in Microsoft Outlook 2000	$14.95
1-879399-80-6	Quick Course® in Microsoft Outlook 98	$14.95
1-58278-004-8	Quick Course® in Microsoft PowerPoint 2000	$14.95
1-879399-72-5	Quick Course® in Microsoft PowerPoint 97	$14.95
1-879399-33-4	Quick Course® in PowerPoint 4	$14.95
1-58278-007-2	Quick Course® in Microsoft Publisher 2000	$14.95
1-58278-000-5	Quick Course® in Microsoft Windows 2000	$15.95
1-879399-81-4	Quick Course® in Microsoft Windows 98	$15.95
1-879399-34-2	Quick Course® in Windows 95	$14.95
1-879399-14-8	Quick Course® in Windows 3.1	$14.95
1-879399-22-9	Quick Course® in Windows for Workgroups	$14.95
1-879399-64-4	Quick Course® in Windows NT Workstation 4	$16.95